Who's Flying Your Plane?

How to master the controls of your life

Emma R McNally

Updated First Edition

Published by Emma R McNally
Edited by Charlotte Noon

Text copyright © Emma R McNally, 2023

ISBN – 13: 979 8-8410-6647-7

DEDICATION

This book is dedicated to Shaun, my soul mate ...
I love you.

CONTENTS

ACKNOWLEDGEMENTS

Firstly, I want to thank Shaun, my husband, for his love, kindness and constant support in this and my other projects in life. You are my one and only and I love and really appreciate you.

I want to thank Richard Bandler and John Grinder, who were the originators of NLP. Without their inquisitive minds, I certainly wouldn't be where I am today. I also want to thank those NLP legends and trainers who have shared their knowledge, wisdom and insights – those who helped me start my personal NLP journey (Jessica Reed-Robbins) through to those who have supported me along the way (Melody and Joe Cheal). Thank you also to all those I work collaboratively with, especially Karen and Kash Falconer at ANLP, Lynn Robinson in Canada and Elizabeth Everington – you are all legends!

I also want to thank the NLP community in Essex – my incredible students who have learnt how to use NLP to create amazing lives for themselves. I love each and every one of you and am grateful to have had the opportunity to share NLP with you.

A huge thank you to Charlotte Noon, my wonderful editor, who has helped make this book a reality and to Rachel Barclay for your feedback. Also, thank you to Ross Willsher, my photographer.

Finally, I want to thank my Mum – my most senior student, even though she is young at heart! I am so proud to have you as part of my life and my business. Thank you for your tireless proof-reading ability! I love you.

FOREWORD

We are delighted to have been invited to write this foreword for *Who's Flying Your Plane?*, an easy and accessible introduction to the magical world of NLP!

As CEO and COO of ANLP, we already know what a huge, positive difference NLP can make in so many areas. We are already committed to ensuring NLP professionals, like Emma, are able to share their skills and knowledge more widely and *Who's Flying Your Plane?* is a brilliant starting point for your NLP journey. The clear explanations and relatable examples will stand you in good stead throughout your life, even if you only ever apply your understanding to your own future experiences.

The metaphor of *Who's Flying Your Plane?* is instantly relatable. Whether you read this as the pilot, a passenger or, as Emma says in the introduction, you 'need the keys to open the hold of the plane to look inside to find your answers', all perspectives are covered. In this way, the reader can gain greater awareness of what is happening within themselves and how they might make their own choices and take action for positive change. NLP is such a powerful set of tools to equip yourself with and all the NLP skills you can add to the toolbox will enrich and enhance your life experiences.

This is a delightful read because Emma explains each of the basic NLP techniques, including why they are important and how they work – filled with practical exercises and tips as well as clear explanations with many examples, what more could anyone want when starting their journey in NLP? Emma quite correctly focuses on the communication model in the first instance because understanding this is one of the keys to understanding NLP … and then follows up by exploring many of the other underlying models of NLP.

That's part of the brilliance of this book. You may get the feeling that Emma is holding your hand, looking you in the eye and talking directly to your brain, your heart, your gut and your senses... all of your senses, allowing you to connect with what she is saying on whatever level you need to connect on. Then Emma, metaphorically, sits you down and makes sure you have understood everything. Such is the warmth and compassion of her language, it's possible to believe that she is in the room with you: talking to you, encouraging you, checking in, waiting for your (internal) positive response so she can move on to the next point.

NLP has so much to offer everyone, regardless of the stage they have reached in their lives, career or status. Creating a book which is conversational and accessible means opening up the world of NLP to so many more people who may be just curious ... and this is definitely the book to feed that curiosity and leave you wanting more ... which you get, because all of these models and techniques are covered in Part One of the book.

You then move on to Part Two, which is more about taking what you have learned and actually integrating it into your own life. When Karen first discovered NLP, many years ago, it was because someone recommended it to her, saying it was one of the few things that had stuck with them and they had been able to apply it in real life. For Kash, NLP has given him the ability to use the tools to tweak and change himself in many areas of business and life.

Part Two is really what will empower you to develop, change or transform your life where *you* want to ... at your own pace, in your own way. It allows you to know *exactly* who's flying your plane ... as long as you engage and take the steps forward with Emma's book as your guide ... all the way through to Chapter 16 – creating your exciting future.

We have both done this for ourselves and created our own exciting futures, thanks largely to NLP and the difference it has made to our lives. Follow Emma's guidance throughout this book and you will continue that journey for yourself.

Maybe one day you will be joining ANLP as one of those NLP

professionals that Emma refers to in the book ... and if you prefer to use NLP for your own personal journey, then you can find Emma, along with all the other trained NLP professionals on the Association website.

Karen and Kash Falconer

CEO and COO of ANLP International CIC, the Association for NLP Professionals

www.anlp.org

INTRODUCTION

Does your life sometimes feel turbulent? Does it often seem as though one minute you are gliding along smoothly and the next you are being tossed around by events outside your control?

Do you spend a lot of time worrying and agonising over situations? It can be easy to get stuck in a vicious circle with these thoughts going round and round in your mind. Not only does this take up time and effort, which could be better spent, it can leave you feeling discombobulated, frustrated and stressed.

What if you could learn how to think differently so that you could thrive during these situations? To have a different perspective on what is happening? To have the strategies and tools to enable you to change your approach, which will change your outcome and enable you to be more successful?

Well, that is what this book is all about. It is designed to help you navigate through life's ups and downs with greater ease. It is in your influence to do this. You just need the keys to open the hold of your plane and look inside to find your answers.

I will provide some key thoughts, insights and tools to help you to:
- understand how you create your own reality
- model the techniques of those who are exceptional in their field so that you too can become exceptional
- learn some amazing tools to get through challenging situations with greater ease, wisdom and clarity
- become an even better version of yourself and tap into the unlimited potential that you have within you
- get back into the pilot's seat of your life and have more choice
- Take back those controls and enjoy the flight!

I believe that every person deserves to learn about NLP (neuro-linguistic programming); it has been one of the best kept secrets for many years ... it is now time to change all that. It is time for every person, no matter their upbringing, situation or age to learn these powerful techniques and to become masters of their own destiny.

What can you expect?

This book is a practical NLP guide to help you to understand what is happening around you, the reasons why you do what you do and, more importantly, what you can do about it, especially if you are not currently getting the outcomes you want.

I will give you techniques and strategies to help you make the changes you desire as I share my knowledge of NLP with you.

I believe that the most powerful way to experience NLP is via live training although reading around the subject is a great start. One of my students recently observed that reading about NLP is like reading a cookery book – you may enjoy reading it and looking at the pictures but it is a poor second to actually eating the food! The power comes when you apply what you have learnt and I would always recommend you find yourself an accredited NLP course or a certified NLP professional to see maximum results.

For those of you who know about NLP, this book just scratches the surface. NLP is a huge and fascinating subject, continuously evolving as our understanding of neuroscience and psychology advances. We all need to start somewhere, however, and that is what this book provides: a starting point or a great way to refresh and reflect on your journey to date.

It should be noted that this book is for educational purposes only. NLP is not a substitution for professional medical advice or intervention and it is recommended that you seek medical advice for any medical conditions.

The book is divided into two parts:

Part One – The fundamental principles, concepts and strategies of NLP to prepare you for take-off

Part Two – How to enjoy the flight of your life by living NLP from day to day.

Reading Part One first will give you the basic knowledge before putting it into practice in Part Two; however, you can also just delve straight into Part Two if you choose – this book is all about choice, after all!

Throughout the book there will be:

 NLP techniques and activities for you to do

 A summary of key learnings at the end of each chapter.

So, fasten your seatbelt and let's get started ...

PART ONE – GETTING READY FOR TAKE-OFF

CHAPTER 1 – WHAT IS NLP?

Neuro-linguistic programming, or NLP for short, was created in the 1970's in America by John Grinder and Richard Bandler. They modelled people who were excellent in their field: Milton Erickson (arguably the greatest hypnotherapist of our time), Virginia Satir (a family therapist) and Fritz Perls (a Gestalt Therapist).

By studying their work extensively, Grinder and Bandler noticed patterns and models of language that these experts were using. They subsequently applied these models with many clients and discovered that they achieved the same results as the experts, simply through using the same language patterns. This was how NLP started – by modelling experts in their field, by observing what was happening and being curious and inquisitive to find answers to enable us to have greater success in our lives today.

What does NLP mean?

The 'neuro' element refers to our neurological system which regulates how we function and by applying some basic neuroscience, we can start to understand how and why we do what we do.

The 'linguistic' part refers to language. When we talk about language, it is much wider than just words; we are talking about tonality, body language, facial expressions and our internal dialogue (self-talk and thoughts). In fact, we are talking about every way in which we communicate. You are communicating at the moment, even if you are not consciously intending to!

The 'programming' part refers to change. Remember that NLP was originally created in the 1970's when computer programming was new and trendy. What we are talking about is how we can re-programme patterns of behaviours and beliefs when they are no longer serving us.

Therefore, putting the three elements together, NLP is all about understanding why we do what we do, how we do it and how this creates our own unique experience of life. We can then change those things that aren't working for us by using NLP techniques and NLP language so that we can be the best version of ourselves and have better relationships with others.

The result: it enables us to have the life we desire, rather than the one we are experiencing by default.

Robert Dilts, one of the great legends within the NLP field, defines NLP as 'the study of the structure of subjective experience'. Every experience we have is subjective and with NLP we can learn how we have created that reality and how we can change it, should we wish to.

As you are starting to realise, NLP is powerful stuff and can be used in all areas of your life – from personal to professional, and everything in between. I love it because it isn't just a theory ... it gives us choice as well as real, practical things you can do to make change happen in your life, which are supported by neuroscience, modelling excellence and research.

CHAPTER 2 – HOW YOU CREATE YOUR REALITY

One of the biggest insights for me when I began to learn about NLP was that everybody's version of reality is subjective and different. For example, if I made a cup of coffee and a number of people took a sip, each person would have a different experience. Some may find it too hot … some too sweet … some not sweet enough. I am sure you are thinking that this is nothing new; however, what we tend to overlook is the application of this principle in wider or more complex situations. We understand how this works in terms of preferences for food, drink, art or music but what about when we take it a step further?

When we look at any situation, we are looking at it through our own perspective or version of reality, yet how often do we stop to consider this when solving a problem at work or during a disagreement or a political debate? In these instances, it is all too easy to believe that our version of reality is the correct and only truth, rather than realising that our view is just one of many and subjective.

This is easy to understand when we think of our brains as projectors rather than cameras. Rather than our brains taking a 'snapshot' or photo of reality, we are continuously projecting our internal map of the world (thoughts, feelings and beliefs) onto the situation, which impacts our attitude towards it.

In this chapter, we will be starting to explore and understand how we create our own version of reality (model of the world) and discover why it is different from someone else's.

Why is this important?

In conversations, it can be easy to slip straight into a judgement: 'I'm right, you're wrong' or 'You're right, I'm wrong.'

When we understand that our reality is subjective, personal and unique to us and that the person with whom we are communicating has their own unique and potentially different version of reality, then rather than being judgemental, we can approach their viewpoint with curiosity and genuine interest. It can ease our frustration. We become much more tolerant, compassionate and understanding. Issues such as racism and sexism can dissolve as we come from a place of understanding and curiosity with the knowledge that every person is unique and different.

Having this viewpoint also helps us to avoid becoming stuck in our own version of reality, where we could be missing opportunities to learn and to stretch. Instead, we can have a richer life experience. By being curious and genuinely interested in a different perspective, it enables us to stretch our map of the world, explore new horizons and become wiser, more tolerant, and flexible. We will see later why this is so important, especially in our modern world.

As the Spiritual guide Rumi's beautiful poem *A Great Wagon* quotes:

'Out beyond ideas of wrongdoing and rightdoing, there is a field. I'll meet you there.'

The NLP Communication Model, which we are going to be exploring next, underpins these principles and enables us to understand how we create our reality: this subjective experience of life. It can enable you to have a richer, fuller more peaceful life where you become curious and open rather than having to always prove that you are right. This is key to successful relationships and will provide you with a whole new way of living, should you wish. It certainly did for me.

The NLP Communication Model

The NLP Communication Model is, in my view, the lynch pin of our understanding of relationships and communication. It is the way we create our subjective experience. I like to use it as a framework upon which to hang tools and insights of NLP.

Here is the diagram:

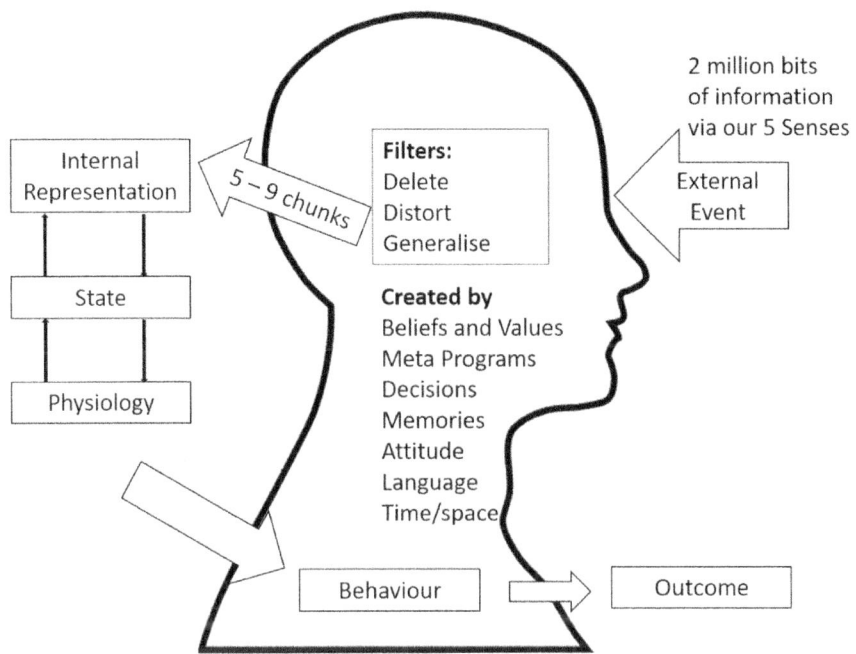

Why is it so important? Well, it explains the reasons why people (you and me included) behave in the way that they do and the basis of how communication can sometimes be misunderstood.

For example, have you ever had a time when you thought you made yourself clear and then afterwards it turned out that the person with whom you were speaking had a different interpretation of what you were saying?

Or maybe you received an extreme and unexpected response to something you said?

Or maybe you thought you had understood what someone had said to you and later found that you hadn't?

If any of the above situations are familiar to you, or you just want to understand your own or other people's responses better, then this model gives you that explanation. The more we understand what is happening when we process information, the better we can become at learning to change what isn't working for us and become curious as to how to have better relationships with others and communicate more effectively.

We take in information through our senses

The first thing to appreciate is how we take in information from the outside world through our five senses, known as either representational systems or modalities in NLP. These are visual (what we see), auditory (what we hear), kinaesthetic (what we feel), olfactory (what we smell) and gustatory (what we taste).

At any one time, we are being bombarded with millions of pieces of information. Just take a moment to look around you now – what can you see? Look at the detail of the items in front of you – the colour, texture and shape. This is all information that we are taking in through our visual sense.

Now be quiet for a minute and listen – what are you hearing? I'm sitting in my garden right now whilst writing this. When I am typing, I know that I am shutting out sounds around me. When I stop and listen, I then notice voices in the background, the odd car driving along the road, someone mowing their lawn in the distance and birds singing. Again, lots of information, some of which we may not be consciously aware of.

Kinaesthetic awareness refers to feelings and touch – whether something is hard or soft; the temperature; whether you are hot or cold; the air on your face; your emotional state; whether you are happy or sad and even whether you are feeling full or hungry. When we talk about kinaesthetic awareness, we can be talking about any feelings or sensations.

We also take in information via smell and taste – maybe it is the smell of dinner cooking, or the taste in your mouth from the last drink that you had.

The conscious and unconscious mind

We all have both a conscious and unconscious mind (thankfully!) as both are super important in terms of how we function as humans.

Our conscious mind is the part of our brain where we are actively thinking and making conscious decisions – for many of us it feels like the dominant part of the brain that we are listening to the majority of the time. Our unconscious mind is the part that is doing everything else! Our unconscious mind stores all our memories and wisdom and runs our actual physical system. It remembers to breathe for example, regulates our blood pressure, ensures our heart beats, enables our hair to grow and so on – all rather useful! It all happens simultaneously without us consciously knowing. This is great because otherwise we would have to consciously remember to breathe, and our systems would have to take it in turns to perform each function - make our nails grow and then digest our food, for example.

The conscious mind is like the pilot of a plane – consciously making decisions, giving directions, thinking logically and sequentially, whereas the unconscious mind is like the crew. The crew need direct and clear instructions from the pilot (the conscious mind); however, they run the plane, feed the passengers, load the luggage, fill the fuel, give the safety briefing and so much more (like the unconscious mind).

We need them both and they both play incredibly important roles in our lives. Our conscious mind asks the questions whereas the unconscious mind already has the answers – we just need to communicate with our unconscious mind more easily, especially when we want to feel a greater sense of wholeness.

If we operate just at the conscious level, we can achieve a level of success; however real greatness comes from alignment between both minds and the ability to tap into our own wisdom and resources to enable a more fulfilling and enriched life.

Let's take an example of how this works in practice. Have you ever learnt anything new? Think of the first time you used a new smart phone. You probably had to focus consciously on everything you were doing – how to unlock it, how to take a photo or check your emails. Then after a while, you find you can do it without thinking – on 'auto-pilot' where your unconscious mind is doing it for you. You don't have to consciously think about it. That is your unconscious mind at work. After a while, you may even notice that it comes so automatically to you that you consciously forget how to do it! Have you ever asked an expert, for example, how they do what they do? They may struggle to explain it as it 'just comes naturally!'

Filters

Let's now go back to our NLP Communication Model.

As you now know, we are being bombarded with millions of pieces of information at any one moment via our senses. According to Cognitive Load Theory, we can only consciously process 7 + or – 2 chunks of information at any one time. If we are like Einstein, we could be taking in 9 bits of information, but for the rest of us (especially before coffee in the morning), we are more likely to be closer to the 5 mark!

This explains the reason why, if you go to the bar to order drinks for a large group of friends, by the time you have got halfway through the order, you have probably forgotten some of it ... was it beer or wine that Bert wanted?

Just think about that for a moment – that's a lot of information. So, what do we do with it all? How do we get from millions of pieces of information down to between 5 and 9 chunks? How do we sort out what we focus on and what bits we ignore? Well, we do it unconsciously by using three main filters called Generalisation, Distortion and Deletion.

Let's explore our filters:

Generalisations are those things that we 'lump together' and put into categories to make our lives easier. In other words, we take one occurrence (sometimes more) and extrapolate it to create a belief or category of experiences. It saves us learning everything from scratch every time we see something new. For example, if you have ever been with a young child when they are learning, you will notice how generalisations are created. You show them a cat and explain that 'this is what a cat looks like.' 'Cat!' they exclaim, to your delight. You are then out and about and they see a dog. 'Cat,' they say and you say, 'No, that's a dog,' and show them another cat. This goes on for a while until they know what a cat looks like and from then on – whether the cat is big, small, whatever colour or breed - they know that a cat is a cat!

This is how generalisations are formed. We download information and learnings from others – some helpful and others less so.

We have all created multiple categories for many things, all of which we refer to as generalisations. Now this is great as it stops us from having to relearn everything from scratch – it gives us a short cut as it were. If we did not do this, we would have to learn what a chair was each and every time we saw a slightly different chair! It is very useful to have the generalisation filter, especially for inanimate objects.

Think for a moment about generalisations you have formed … about driving, about people, about what is right or wrong, about how you should behave, about yourself and the world around you. The list is endless.

Many of these generalisations are helpful and some, as mentioned, may be less so. Imagine you think that all xyz drivers are idiots and then you meet a person you really like who drives an xyz car. This generalisation may impact on your relationship with them and your behaviour towards them.

A great clue to discovering the generalisations you or others have formed is to listen to the language that they use. Listen out for the words, 'always', 'never' and 'should' – these often indicate generalisations.

Generalisations can also indicate beliefs; we go through the same process to create our core beliefs, which impact on the way that we view ourselves, our lives and how we create our reality. The psychologist, Piaget, identified that before the age of 7, we download our beliefs (generalisations) and values from those around us - our parents, teachers and carers. By the age of 7, we have already created our fundamental values and beliefs. We carry these with us throughout our lives and we then distort and delete information to meet those beliefs. Beliefs can be so strong that they can impact on our motivation.

An example could be if a person doesn't believe they are good enough. They may not give new things a go and they may miss opportunities. Even when they do undertake a new challenge, there may always be that niggle at the back of their mind in terms of whether they are good enough to make the opportunity work. If, however, they believe they are good enough, then the experience is likely to be very different – they are more likely to see and take advantage of opportunities.

The great news is that if you have any beliefs that aren't working for you, NLP gives you the tools to enable you to change them, should you want to. We will be covering changing beliefs later on in the book.

The deletion filter, as its name suggests, is all about how we unconsciously delete information – it has also been called the sanity filter, as it is about avoiding information overload.

Take a look at your surroundings right now and notice how many white things you can see. Count them up quickly. Got a figure? Great, now without looking, how many blue things were there?

Have another look around – were you right?

When you looked around again, you probably noticed many more blue things than you remembered. Why? Because you had deleted them – you were looking for something else and so you didn't see them.

Have you ever received a message from a friend saying they saw you whilst out in town but you didn't acknowledge them? This is your deletion filter at work. You were probably busy chatting or thinking about something else and therefore didn't consciously notice them

Maybe you have lost your keys and have hunted high and low and then came back to the very first place you looked, and there they were ... again, the deletion filter is at play!

The final filter is the **distortion filter** which has also been called the creativity filter. This is how innovations come into being – by distorting existing things to create something new. For example, when I was at school, we had blackboards and chalk (I know, that really ages me). The electronic white boards that are now found in schools are a distortion of that ... a much more sophisticated version, I grant you!

Many experiments have been conducted to demonstrate this filter. For example, Gordon Stephenson undertook the Five Monkeys Experiment. He had five monkeys in a cage and at the top of the cage was a ladder, leading to a hatch where the keeper would place bananas. The first time that the monkeys were fed, they all raced up the ladder to the hatch and the keeper showered them with icy water. After a while, the monkeys learnt to not go up the ladder to get the bananas. Gradually, new monkeys were introduced to the cage. By then, the keeper had stopped showering them with water, but the monkeys still didn't climb up the ladder because they had learnt not to – they repeated this pattern. It even got to the point where there were no original monkeys left in the cage, yet the monkeys still didn't go up the ladder. This is the distortion filter at play. We continue to follow the same patterns we have learned.

For example, imagine if every time you were nice to a particular person, they replied unkindly. After a little while, even when they did say something nice to you, you would distort what they were saying and believe that they were being unkind because you would be so used to following this pattern.

How our filters work together

Firstly, I should reiterate that these filters work at an unconscious rather than a conscious level. In other words, we generalise, delete and distort without being consciously aware that we are doing so.

Our brains, in essence, are like sorting offices; information comes in and we delete, distort and generalise it to avoid information overload and to make sense of the information from our perspective. Imagine your brain as a big recycling centre; items come in and they go through the filters – anything that is non-recyclable will be binned (deleted); it will then go through the next filter in terms of whether it is paper, card or glass and then be separated into categories (generalisation). Then there will be some left over items which are questionable; for example, those drink cartons which are cardboard on the outside and plastic on the inside (in the UK there are different rules around these depending on where you live!). We are then likely to distort and either put it in one category or the other.

The same goes for the events that we are processing through our filters; the information comes in and we apply all three filters to a greater or lesser extent to the event.

A great example of how these filters work together is a case of a couple who were having relationship issues. The man's issue (belief/generalisation) was that his wife never said anything nice about him. As the session progressed, the wife mentioned something that she really appreciated about her husband. The coach paused the session and asked the husband whether he had heard what his wife had just said. He responded that he hadn't (deletion filter). The coach asked her to repeat what she had said. He then replied that he had noticed what she had said this time; however, he remarked that 'she was only saying it because he [the coach] was there' (distortion filter).

So, you can start to see the power of these filters and how important our beliefs truly are; the question is, are they supporting us or not? I knew someone who believed that he was average and not good enough – this filtered through into all experiences in his life – work, family, friends and hobbies. When he did do something well, he would either ignore it (delete it – again not necessarily consciously, he just didn't notice) or when it was brought to his attention, he would brush it off as a fluke or a 'one off'. He would even look for other external factors which would support his belief that he was average and tell himself stories such as 'well, it was very favourable weather that day,' or 'anyone would have been able to make that shot'.

When we have a strong belief, we go through our life gathering information to prove and reinforce it – this is known as protecting our map of the world.

These filters become the lens through which we view life and indeed create our own reality. I will always remember one cruise we went on. We had a great time and met a couple in the airport who were moaning about what a terrible ship it was. We got chatting and it turned out that they were on the exact same holiday as us. They were creating their own reality by distorting and deleting information to meet their generalisation that the holiday was awful. We were doing the exact same thing (distorting and deleting information to meet our generalisation); however, we were creating our reality that the holiday was great. Remember, rather than it being about who is right or wrong, it is about having a different perspective.

How do we form these filters?

We started to create these filters when we were very young, as mentioned earlier. We download our beliefs and values from those around us. Life experiences can also shape these filters. For example, if you had a bad meal at a restaurant, you are likely to create a generalisation that it is a poor restaurant. That may be the case … or maybe the chef was off sick and someone else was just helping out? Maybe you are waiting for a bus and it's late – you then create the generalisation that the bus service is poor and you'll never use it again. Maybe it is poor or maybe there was a road accident or the traffic was particularly busy that day, which caused the delay.

Can you see how our experiences can create these filters and start to shape our map of the world? We are constantly generalising, deleting and distorting information to support the map which we have created – it is an evolving thing. The good news is that even those beliefs that we downloaded as young children can be changed so that we can create a different reality for ourselves.

These filters have also been created from our values – what is important to us, our memories (things that have happened previously), the language that was used (from tonality through to actual words), meta programs (the patterns of behaviour that create the structure of our personality), experiences and attitudes.

As you can see therefore, every person's experience is different; everyone has a unique set of filters which thereby creates their own unique subjective view of reality – the lens through which they see life.

Let's put it all together

An external event happens. You take in information through your senses. You then filter the information (deletion, distortion and generalisation) so you are left with 7+or-2 chunks of information. You then create an internal representation in your mind (a movie in your mind) which helps you to create meaning around the event. The meaning you have created impacts on your state (how you feel) which is also impacted by your physiology. This is why when you are tired, you are more likely to react in a less resourceful way to a situation than when you are full of energy. This then impacts on how you behave (what you say or do).

This behaviour is the part that others see – all the rest is a chain reaction that has happened at the speed of light, unconsciously. This then impacts your outcome and whether it is a good or less than helpful experience for you.

In shorthand: an event happens, you respond and then there is an outcome (Event + Response = Outcome).

The great news is that even if the event is outside your control, you can choose your response, which then impacts your outcome.

For example, if someone cuts a person up on the road (external event) and they filter the information and interpret the person as rude or ignorant, they then behave by hooting their horn. The resulting outcome is that they feel annoyed and are left feeling unhappy about the whole experience.

However, when they change their response, the outcome can be very different ... even though the event is the same. The meaning they take from the event could be that maybe the driver was in a rush, or maybe they hadn't seen them there (deletion – most of us have done this inadvertently at some point). The response could be to wave the driver through and the outcome for them would be to feel good about what had happened rather than annoyed.

Can you see how just changing our response can change the outcome for the better? This is how we can take back control over our outcomes and our lives and start to create the reality that we want to have. After all, we don't know whether they really didn't see us or if they were being rude. At the end of the day, usually the only person who is upset by the road incident is you, not the other person ... so what do you want? To feel annoyed and upset or resourceful and in control? The choice is yours.

It is also really important to notice how everyone's filters are different – we are all unique and everyone has had a different experience of life. Even if the same event happens to every person, the way that they delete, distort or generalise the information is unique to them as this is based on their memories, attitude, experience, language and timing, amongst other factors.

This is why two people, who have seen exactly the same incident, may notice different things and create different meanings from it. Everyone's version of reality is slightly different because it is created by our own unique experience and interpretation of said experience.

Let me give you an example. We had an extension to our house a good number of years ago and when we were nearing completion, the plasterers started their work. One day, they left the backing on the wall exposed and I walked into the room and had a very strong adverse reaction to it, almost a panic attack (this was before I learnt about NLP). The reason was that when I was a little girl, I had broken my leg and it wasn't a straight-forward situation – with talk about operations, a benign tumour and the like. Seeing that plaster took me back to that memory of having my leg in plaster. My reaction was one that, from the external view, would have been unexpected and disproportionate to the situation (we call this an anchor in NLP and we look at this in more detail in Chapter 6). However, from my perspective it had brought back all those memories of being alone and frightened in hospital. My husband's reaction to the plaster backing was totally different (even though he had broken his arm when he was a child). Why? Because he hadn't had that exact same experience as me and so the meaning he took from the event was different.

So, if someone is reacting in a different way to the way you expect, become curious about what is happening to them rather than judgemental. We don't know what is going on in their lives right now or what has happened historically to cause them to act in that way. We are always perceiving life from our map of the world rather than theirs.

I used to work in insurance and we would get all sorts of interesting claims through; witness statements would often differ, even when they were all present at the same incident. With this knowledge, you can now understand why this is; each individual will be distorting, deleting and generalising the situation based on their own map of the world. It will also be dependent on their physiology, state and the resulting behaviour. To add another level of complexity, when they went back to think about the situation afterwards and write their witness statement, they would go through their filters yet again. Have you noticed this? When someone retells stories over and over, it can get more dramatic every time ... well, this is the reason why.

So, what is true? What is reality? Well, we are always going to get an individual's version of reality – not reality itself. This can be really useful to understand in terms of relationships – it isn't about being right, it is about being curious as to the other person's perspective. When you take out the blame and criticism and become curious, this gives you a new fresh perspective on others and their lives – and perhaps even a more tolerant one.

In general, people tend to judge themselves by their intention and others by their behaviour. As we now understand what is going on to process this information, we can start to realise that people are not their behaviours – this is just a moment in time. Have you ever been short with someone or snappy and later regretted it? Well, that is what we are talking about. We are all human and our behaviours are a reflection of what is going on for that person in that particular time or space. We can then become curious as to what is happening for them. From an NLP perspective, if our behaviour is something that we don't like, we can change it – we do have choice. That is the great news – we can have choice over what is happening so that we can start to create a better version of reality.

This whole process comes together to create our map of the world – our own unique version of reality and our filters of deletion, distortion and generalisation are there to protect our model of the world. If, however, your outcomes aren't as you anticipate or want, by changing your filters, beliefs, interpretation/meaning, states and behaviour, you can change the outcome for yourself and start to stretch your map of the world in a positive way.

The rest of this book will give you some techniques as to how you can start to make these changes.

Key Learnings

The key learnings from this chapter are:

1. NLP Communication Model helps us to understand how we create our version of reality.
2. All experience is subjective and we can become curious as to what is going on with others to enable us to have better relationships.
3. We take in millions of pieces of information at any one time; however, we can only consciously process 7 +or- 2 chunks of information.
4. We have three main filters created through our own unique experiences, to reduce this information:
    a. Generalisations (these are our beliefs)
    b. Distortion
    c. Deletion.
5. Once we have filtered this information, we generate meaning through creating an internal representation of our experience.
6. This impacts on how we feel about the experience (i.e. our state), which is impacted by our physiology (and our physiology impacts on our emotions too).
7. Once all of the above steps have taken place, we then behave (act or say something) based on this internal processing.
8. Finally, this impacts on our outcome.
9. The whole process happens at an unconscious level and at the speed of light!
10. By changing our response (filters, states and behaviours), this can change our outcome and we can start to become the architect of our lives by design, rather than accepting life by default.

CHAPTER 3 – SETTING UP FOR SUCCESS

Have you noticed how some people seem to glide through life easily, despite the hassles and difficulties they face? Even when life throws them curve balls, they bounce back or don't even appear to notice what's happening. However, if the exact same thing had happened to someone else, they might have had a very different experience.

What is it about those people that enables them to have that level of success? What are they thinking or doing differently to be able to move through their life so much more easily than others?

In this chapter, we are going to uncover their secret.

As you already know, NLP was created by Richard Bandler and John Grinder, who modelled people who were exceptional in their field, so that we can become excellent in ours.

In this chapter we are going to be looking at:
- the presuppositions of NLP: the underlying principles which successful people live by
- the difference between living 'at cause' and living 'at effect'
- how to take responsibility for our own outcomes
- how to tackle those things that can pull us back from what we really want.

These elements are critical to consider before we make any changes: they are the foundations that need to be laid to achieve greatness in our lives.

The presuppositions of NLP

The presuppositions of NLP are principles that underpin NLP and help us become more successful. Let's look at each of them in turn:

1. Have respect for the other person's map of the world

We looked at the NLP Communication Model in Chapter 2 and how we create our map of the world (our version of reality). As you know, each map of the world is unique to that individual.

People who have greater success in their lives have respect for the other person's map or version of reality. Rather than being judgemental, they are curious and respectful and seek to understand differences.

This understanding that another person is operating from their own map which is different to our own (not right or wrong, just different), changes our interactions with them. The pressure to be right or wrong is lifted. We seek to support them, rather than blame them.

As you adopt this presupposition of NLP, you will discover that your life becomes easier. When people act or react in an unexpected way, you will begin to notice that this is because their map of the world is different to yours.

Let me give you an example. Before I learnt about NLP, I had a minor operation. Two years prior to the operation, my Dad had been given too much anaesthetic on the operating table and I formed a fearful belief that I was going to die during my operation.

On the day of my operation, the surgeon and anaesthetist calmly and rationally started to explain the procedure. I was in floods of tears and my blood pressure soared. They sent me home, telling me to return in a month when I had 'sorted myself out.'

Well, during that month, I learnt NLP. I learnt how to change that unhelpful belief and get rid of the fear so that when I went back to have the operation, it was a different experience. I was laughing and joking – they hardly recognised me! In fact, as they put me under the anaesthetic, I was telling them about a holiday in Las Vegas and woke up in recovery mid-sentence! It was a completely different experience.

What had changed? I was in charge of my own response. Previously, I did not even know that I had the power to make these changes.

Let's look at it from a map of the world perspective. That surgeon probably thought I was being completely irrational; however, she didn't know that the fear had been created by what had happened to my Dad two years previously. She didn't know what was going on in my map of the world. To her, this was just another day, a minor operation and I was just the next patient. She had no idea what was going on for me.

People won't always tell you what is going on for them. By being curious and supportive though, you can make it easier for them to tell you if they want to. In the language and relationship section, we will talk more about how you can do this in a way that supports the other person – by going around to their side first, having empathy and asking clean questions.

As previously mentioned, often we judge a person by their behaviour (the part we can easily see) ... not their intention (which is often more concealed). This presupposition turns this on its head, enabling us to better understand the other person.

2. People are not their behaviours

In NLP, we focus on changing ourselves because we can't change others (however much we might want to try!)

We tend to judge others on their behaviour as this is what we see, hear or feel. We all make snappy remarks sometimes or say things we regret but this is just a snapshot in time – it isn't who we are.

So, rather than judging people solely on their behaviours, it is about realising that we are all so much more than just what we say or do; we are rich and complex individuals.

3. People are doing the best they can with the resources they have available and every behaviour is motivated by a positive intention.

Let's break this one down as at first it seems quite long and wordy!

Let's start with the idea that every behaviour has a positive intention, even when the behaviour itself seems less than positive. The behaviour may not serve a positive intention for others, but it will almost definitely serve a positive intention for us.

There has been much research around this concept both inside and outside of the NLP world. Maslow's Hierarchy of Needs Theory, for example, states that our actions are motivated by certain physiological needs. Only when we have our most basic needs fulfilled (food, drink, warmth, safety and security) do we seek to fulfil the higher-level needs such as love and belonging and self-actualisation.

Glasser's Choice Theory is another model outside NLP which states that everyone at any one time has a fundamental need which our behaviour is seeking to meet (such as love, belonging, fun, power, survival and freedom).

Both of these theories link nicely to this presupposition that our behaviour isn't just behaviour – there is something deeper and more fundamental that is driving what we say and do. So even when our behaviour is unwanted, there is some higher purpose or need that it is looking to fulfil.

Acknowledging that there is a positive intention behind every behaviour is important before making any changes. We need to identify the positive intention of our old behaviours so that we can make sure that the positive intention is still being met, even after we make the change.

For example, I am sure that you have met people who have given up smoking and then instantly moved onto another habit, like eating chocolate. This is because the positive intention that smoking fulfilled is no longer being fulfilled once they quit smoking. Stopping smoking has left a gap – a need – that is no longer being met, so they replace it by eating chocolate.

When we look to make change, therefore, we need to understand what that positive intention is and make sure that any changes we make will satisfy that positive intention – ideally in a healthier or more ecological way.

Activity – Chunking Up

The way to discover the positive intention of any behaviour, is to use a technique called 'chunking up'.

1. **Ask:** What is that behaviour doing for you?

2. Continue to ask this question again and again until you get from a lower-level need such as 'it makes me feel full' for example, to a higher level of feeling 'significant' or 'loved' or 'certain'.

   If you bite your nails for example and you wanted to stop, your questioning might look something like this:
   Question: What does biting your nails do for you?
   Answer: Well, it gives me something to do.
   Question: What does 'it gives me something to do', do for you?
   Answer: It keeps me occupied.
   Question: What does 'it keeps me occupied', do for you?

3. You would then repeat the process until you get to the highest level of intention. You may find that keeping occupied gives you satisfaction or relaxation, which ultimately makes you feel you have a purpose.

4. Once you are at that highest level, then you can do some lateral chunking:

Ask: What else could I do that would meet that higher level positive intention?

Your answers could include talking to a friend, reading a book, cooking or gardening. You can then choose which one or ones would work better for you.

At the moment, we are setting up for success (as the title of the chapter indicates). When we come to Chapter 7, we will be talking about how to change those less than helpful behaviours.

The positive intention is really important because EVERY behaviour is motivated by a positive intention. Even if somebody is doing something that is doing them physical damage or is harmful, it still has a positive intention for them.

If someone self-harms, for example, the positive intention or need this is fulfilling could be about feeling relief or feeling in control. We all have an inherent need to feel in control. The great news is that they can find something else that gives them the same positive intention of feeling in control without causing the harm of the original behaviour.

It is so important to discover the positive intention as without this, we may hinder our success. We might swap eating chocolate with eating celery, for example. On the surface, it looks like a good swap. However, unless celery gives the person the same positive outcome as chocolate, the change won't stick … and I have yet to find anyone for whom eating celery has the same positive outcome as chocolate!

Now let's look at the first part of the presupposition – people are doing the best they can with the resources they have available. We all have times where we feel more resourceful than others. If you are a morning person and you jump out of bed and are feeling great, you are more likely to make good choices than if you are tired after a long week.

Resources also includes knowledge; sometimes we just don't

have the knowledge that we need at that time. In other words, we just don't know any better and therefore our response was the best available to us in that moment.

The presupposition therefore states that we are making the best choices and doing the best we can with the resources we have available at that point in time, which leads nicely onto our next presupposition ...

4. Individuals have all the resources they need to achieve their desired outcomes. There are no unresourceful people, just unresourceful states.

If we label people as 'moody', 'snappy' or 'uncooperative', this creates a generalisation or belief in our map of the world which is less than helpful. By realising that this is just a state they are experiencing at that moment in time, rather than believing that this is how they are all the time, we can become more curious and open to helping and supporting the other person, rather than judging and labelling. Greatness comes from having a flexible approach rather than a rigid set of labels when it comes to relationships.

We are therefore presupposing that every person has all the resources they need to achieve their desired outcome. When I refer to 'resources', I am referring to our emotional state, behaviours, capabilities, skills and ability to ask for help.

It is so much more useful to see people in that way, rather than to see them as helpless or unresourceful.

This is so important because if we view people as unresourceful, then we start to see them as a victim. That's less than helpful as we can go into rescuer mode or (in transactional analysis terms) 'parent' mode. It also means that we are likely to feel sympathy rather than empathy. There's a great image that my friend uses to differentiate between empathy and sympathy. If you imagine a hole in the ground and somebody is in the hole, sympathy is about jumping into the hole with them, meaning both of you are stuck, whereas empathy is about throwing a rope down into the hole to help pull them up. Empathy is about getting alongside somebody and helping to support them through what is happening to them. It puts you in a position to be able to help them create a healthy and supportive environment to make changes.

We all have the resources to achieve our desired outcomes even if we may sometimes need some help to find them.

We look at how to change our emotions and states in Chapter 6, so that if you are feeling unresourceful, you can change to feel more resourceful to move forward more easily.

5. The map is not the territory

As you know from the NLP Communication Model, the way we perceive the world stems from our own personal version of reality – it isn't reality itself.

This idea that 'the map is not the territory' can be illustrated by Google Maps. In street view mode, you can feel like you're walking along the road even though you're not actually there. You could be looking at the houses, the street, the trees and the cars; it's not actual reality that you're seeing but just a picture of reality – a snapshot in time. It is just a map, not the actual location or territory.

We all have our own version of reality and we constantly distort, delete and generalise information that we see, hear, feel, smell or taste to fit our own map of reality.

In our daily interactions, we make assumptions about what is going on for other people based on our own unique map of the world. It is not necessarily the reality. The same is true all the time when we view life. Rather than having the view that a person was being untruthful, you can now understand that they are just talking from their own map of the world – in other words, they are describing their map (their version of the incident), rather than describing the territory itself.

6. You're in charge of your mind and therefore your results and I'm in charge of my mind and therefore my results.

I love this one as it places the responsibility for each and every one of us firmly at our own door – rather than pointing at others to allocate blame. This idea that we are in charge of ourselves and our minds is so powerful.

This fits nicely with the equation introduced earlier in the book:

Event + Response = Outcome

You are in charge of your mind and therefore your outcome.

Even if something happens that's outside your control, the way you respond to it is within your control – nobody else can 'make' you feel or do anything. You can choose how you feel, how you behave, what you say and what you do. This is really empowering as it removes that feeling that someone else is controlling you.

On the flip side, we must also realise that we cannot control other people – even if we want to. They are in control of themselves. We can't make them do or be something they don't want to do or be.

In the last century there was an incredibly inspirational man called Viktor Frankl who was in a concentration camp. His family was tortured and murdered and he himself was starved and beaten. He realized that between event and outcome there is a gap and in that gap he could choose his response. Through choosing his response, this had an impact on his outcome; he not only survived, he also inspired so many people through his wisdom.

Another great example is Nelson Mandela – another wise man who realised that no matter what happened to him, the one thing that people couldn't take away was what he thought, how he felt and therefore how he behaved … that sat firmly within his control.

For us, this revelation puts us back in the pilot's seat of our own lives.

We are all accountable and responsible for our actions, thoughts and feelings. We talk about this in a bit more detail later on in this chapter when we talk about living 'at cause' or living 'at effect'.

7. Effective communicators utilise all communication available to them. Resistance is a sign of lack of rapport (insufficient pacing).

The application of this presupposition will help you become exceptional in terms of communication, which is at the heart of all good relationships. For many, relationships (whether with friends, family or work colleagues) are one of the most important parts of life; they make the world go round!

In order to become an exceptional communicator, you need to use all the communication available to you: the words that you use and also how you say those words (your tonality) as well as your body language.

There is a great model created by Albert Mehrabian that looks at congruence within communication. He discovered that only 7% of meaning is derived from the actual words that are said. 38% comes from the tonality and the way that the words are said. 55% of meaning is derived from body language! In order to be congruent in terms of communication, all three need to be aligned.

Effective communicators use all the elements of communication available to them. In NLP, we learn to develop great calibration skills so that we can notice minute differences in facial expressions, body language and tonality. If these three elements don't appear congruent, we can use questioning to find out what's truly going on for the other person. Having these skills, enables us to pick up on even the smallest incongruence.

It is important to avoid generalisations in terms of body language.

For example, when somebody has their arms crossed, we might assume that they are resisting or are disinterested. However, this may not be the case – they may be disinterested or they may just be cold!

Taking this approach will enable you to become an excellent communicator - to get past the labels, to get past the judgements, to get past your map of the world. By being curious rather than judgemental, you can find out what is really going on for the other person and build better relationships.

If there is resistance from another person, we need to communicate in a different way to lower the resistance and ensure our message is understood. The NLP approach is about being flexible and working harder to build rapport so that we can help lower resistance and land our message successfully (and therefore get better outcomes). We talk more about how to build rapport in Chapter 15.

8. The meaning of the communication is the response you get

If the response you get from communicating with someone isn't what you expected it to be, then it is about us taking the responsibility to communicate it in a different way. Their reaction to your communication tells you exactly how they have interpreted your communication – whether it was how you meant it to be received or not.

We need to use our calibration skills and our sensory acuity (i.e. pick up on the detail of the congruence of their reaction) to understand whether we have landed our message successfully.

Often people make statements such as, 'Well I have sent them the email, so they should know' or 'I've told them what I want them to do, so it is up to them now.' Rather than assuming that it is the other person's responsibility to understand, it is more useful to assume that we are responsible for communicating in a way that others will understand. We are the ones that need to be flexible and change our approach to ensure that our message has been understood in the way we intended.

We will be looking at language in Chapter 11 and some ways to change the way we communicate for better outcomes.

9. You cannot not communicate. You are always communicating either verbally or non-verbally.

This means that we are communicating all the time. Even when you are sitting there silently, you are still communicating though your body language and facial expressions.

If you're on a conference call, for example, and you turn off your screen, you are communicating. Think of all the different meanings this could have – it can be easy for somebody to misinterpret your intention.

We tend to mind-read what the other person is meaning. In other words, we think we know what is going on for the other person based on our map of the world. People tend to make judgements based on that other person's reaction, so again it's about curiosity, rather than judgement and picking up on all the elements of communication.

It is also important to realise that other people are also evaluating what we are communicating all the time too, so how are you coming across?

10. All outcomes are achievements. There's no such thing as failure, only feedback.

I love this one as it gives us permission to be creative and to learn new things.

If all our outcomes are achievements, then we can start to look at life through a different lens. If things don't go to plan, it completely changes our outlook when we look at the experience as feedback rather than failure.

There are some amazing examples of incredible innovations by companies and individuals who have lived by this presupposition. Whilst Edison was working on inventing the electric light, a reporter allegedly asked him, 'What is it like to have failed 1,000 times?' Edison answered, 'I didn't fail 1,000 times. The light bulb was an invention with a thousand steps.'

I love that in science when something doesn't go quite to plan, they use the phrase, 'that's interesting!' They become curious and interested to discover what happened and the perceived failure can actually open up some new great innovations and discoveries that previously would not have been uncovered had that thing gone to plan.

Some of the best inventions in life come from this presupposition that there's no such thing as failure.

I love the example of the company that invented post-it notes. Initially, they were looking to create glue. If there is one thing that post-it notes aren't great at, it is their stick-ability! Through that perceived failure, they created a product that is really useful.

So, when things don't go quite to plan, ask yourself what you can learn from this and then move on.

11. The element in the system with the most flexibility will be the catalyst of the system (Law of Requisite Variety - Systems Theory).

This means that in any situation, the most flexible person (in terms of behavioural choices, ways of thinking and approach) will have the most success and control within the system. This links back to our map of the world; if we have a rigid and fixed map of the world and don't look beyond it, then we can become stuck. However, when we can learn to be flexible and curious in our outlook and communications, we can change our behaviours, emotions and beliefs to ultimately be more successful.

During the pandemic restrictions, we saw a great number of

examples of companies that adapted and changed their business model, and enjoyed great success. We also saw those companies who didn't adapt and didn't survive. I knew one cake making company who decided to close rather than adapt due to Covid. At the very same time, another person I knew set up a cake making business and she did really well – the difference was she chose to be flexible and willing to adapt.

Having that flexibility will make your life easier. There is one thing in life we can guarantee: there is always going to be change. So, if we can be the most flexible when faced with change, then this will increase our chances of success.

Activity – applying the presuppositions

1. Have a think about a situation where you weren't as resourceful as you would have liked to have been or a situation that didn't go as well as you thought it should.

2. Then reconsider the situation by applying each of the presuppositions listed above and notice how different the situation looks through these different lenses.

3. Ask yourself:
    *   What could you have done differently with this different perspective?
    *   What are you going to do differently in the future based on these new insights?

I also recommend that you become familiar with these presuppositions and when you come across a situation which is less than easy for you, refer back to this section and ask yourself what presupposition would be useful for you to apply.

We can't change other people and sometimes we can't even change situations ... what we can do, however, is change ourselves and our perspective on life and viewing life through these presuppositions is one of the key ways to do it.

Living 'at cause' or living 'at effect'.

In NLP, as mentioned previously, we are encouraged to take accountability and responsibility for our lives.

This is a really important concept because it puts you back in control of your life. It gives you the power to make changes, to achieve your goals more easily and improve your life. Taking ownership can be exciting and liberating.

This model is on a continuum with living 'at cause' at one end and living 'at effect' at the other. When you're living 'at cause', you are responsible for yourself and take accountability for what happens to you, including your own emotions. You believe that you can make a difference and that you can make things happen. You are responsible for how you feel, what you do, how you think and you may find yourself asking questions like, 'What can I do to change things?' You look for solutions rather than problems. You may not have chosen this to happen to you, but you ask, 'What can I do to move forward?'

At the other end of the continuum is living 'at effect'. At this end of the continuum, people are giving away their power to others and even to inanimate objects (such as, blaming the internet for 'making' them angry). Inanimate objects may not work sometimes but they don't have the power to go into your brain and to make you feel something! So, if a person is living 'at effect' they are probably asking 'Why me?' or saying, 'It's not fair'.

We are all somewhere on this continuum at different times.

Remember:
Event + Response = Outcome

Those living 'at cause' know that they can choose their response. On the other hand, those who live 'at effect' believe they have no responsibility for any of the elements (event, response or outcome); it is all outside their control, which is a very disempowering place to be and can lead to feelings of helplessness, hopelessness, stress, anxiety and feeling overwhelmed due to the lack of control. People at this end of the continuum feel like they can't do anything about their circumstances. This can lead to the stress response of fight, flight or freeze. This natural response was appropriate years ago when we faced the real threat of sabre-toothed tigers, but this is a disproportionate response to your computer breaking, for example! The realisation that we can choose our response enables us to reduce anxiety and stress and start to look for solutions to move forward.

The other issue around living 'at effect' is that people can be open to emotional manipulation as they feel responsible for other people's emotions rather than their own. So, if they don't believe that they are responsible for themselves then unscrupulous people could manipulate them from an emotional perspective. For example, if they feel responsible for other people's emotions but not their own, you may hear them saying, 'I can't do that because Joe won't be happy' or maybe a salesman would say, 'Well if you don't get this fixed then you'll be letting your children down or people will think you are a failure.'

In essence, living 'at effect' is like leaving your control panel open for others to press your buttons.

The language we use gives us clues as to where we are on the continuum of living 'at cause' or 'at effect'. If we say that 'Bert made me angry,' this indicates that we are living 'at effect'. On the other hand, when we say, 'I am choosing to react calmly to this situation', we are living 'at cause'.

Start to listen to your own language - what you say about situations to your friends as well as your own internal self-talk. Do things or people 'make you feel something' or do you talk about being responsible for what's happening in your life? For example, if your computer breaks, do you say, 'my computer has made me angry' or do you say, 'I'm feeling frustrated about my computer', knowing that you can have choice over your emotions in order to resolve the situation more successfully.

We will learn how to manage our emotions more easily later in the book. If your computer is broken, for example, feeling calm and resourceful and having choice over your feelings is going to be much more useful than being angry and throwing it across the room!

Another way of discovering whether you are living 'at cause' or 'at effect' is if you find yourself worrying about things outside of your control. Now, I am not saying that you shouldn't do something about issues that you are concerned about; however, worrying without taking any action is not a great way to use your energy. Not only that, you can feel out of control and anxious, which sends negative biochemicals around your body – I talk more about this and the impact on our immune system later on when I talk about psychoneuroimmunology. Rather than worrying about things that are outside your control, shift your focus to those things that you can influence and change.

Let me give you an example of how this works in real life. A number of years ago, we were on holiday in Egypt when a Russian plane was blown up. We found ourselves stranded in Egypt.

Let's look again at the equation (Event + Response = Outcome) and living 'at cause' or living 'at effect' in response to this. Had we chosen for this event to happen and to be stranded in Egypt? No, absolutely not. However, we were responsible for choosing to be on holiday, so we did need to take some responsibility for being in that situation. The situation wasn't all of our making, but we did have a hand in being there. After all, I did book the tickets, pack the bags and spend 2 weeks in a beautiful resort!

We focused on what we could influence and searched for ways to communicate with people at home. We considered how to keep resourceful and make the best of the situation. We couldn't do anything to change the event but we could manage our response. We knew that the way we reacted to that event would have a ripple effect on other people and also on our eventual outcome of getting home safely and feeling okay about the whole incident.

There were a lot of people in the same situation, some who were blaming the airlines, the travel companies, the authorities – in fact, anyone or anything in close proximity. They certainly were showing signs of extreme stress (hysteria, crying and screaming). This fight, flight or freeze response meant that their outcome was less than positive as they had given away their power and control... living at the 'effect' side of the continuum.

Now I am not saying that this is always easy ... what is important to realise is that by knowing this, we can start to make changes and the more we do it, the easier it will become. So, when we live more 'at cause' and take responsibility for ourselves, then this will start to become a natural and more empowering way to live our lives.

By noticing your language and then asking empowering questions such as, 'how can I resolve this?' or 'how can I move forward?' this will start to enable you to move along the continuum towards the living 'at cause' end where you will be back in the pilot's seat of your life. Knowing that you have responsibility over your response and have choice as to how you react opens up opportunities, gives you the power to make changes and helps you to steer towards a better outcome.

Ecology

When making changes in your life, it's important to consider ecological implications. This means thinking about the consequences of the changes you want to make.

'No man is an island' as the famous quote says. We all live in a world where what we do will impact on others and others' actions impact on us.

When you make changes and apply the tools you will be learning in the rest of the book, it is important to think about what the consequences of those changes are before you make them.

Let me give you an example from my own life. When I set up my own business, there were obviously consequences from moving from a corporate job (with business partners from finance to HR on speed dial and a great team around me) to working on my own in my office with just myself as company! Doing an ecology check in terms of a change of career is about understanding what the consequences are and then managing them accordingly.

Being aware of them, rather than going into a situation blind, is much more helpful. Move forward a good few years and I am still running my own company; however, I have an amazing network of other business owners and I collaborate with a number of other companies and even people in other countries. So, had I thoroughly considered all the consequences of working on my own, I would have still set up my own business and I would have found networks and other groups earlier in that journey to gain support. Thinking about the consequences of what you're going to do in terms of change enables you to plan and manage those consequences more easily.

When you're thinking about the changes that you want to make, you need to think about the consequences (the ecology) of the change and how will it integrate into your life.

- How will life be different?
- What will you see, feel and hear when your life is different?
- How will things be better?
- Is there any way things could be worse by making this change? If so, what would you need to do about that?
- What impact will the change have in terms of your home life, your work life, your family, your friends?

Consider the intended consequences as well as the unintended ones.

Secondary gain

The other element that is important to think about is secondary gain. This is about the unintended (or maybe even unconscious) benefits that the old behaviour is giving you. With the change of career example, the secondary gain could be working from home or flexible hours which meant that you could collect your children from school. Or that you worked with an amazing group of people and you loved the social aspect of work ... will the next job give you that? If not, what else can you do to make sure that this important secondary gain can be met in an alternative way?

Let me give you another example. If somebody was unwell, there could be a secondary gain around time off work, getting flowers or chocolates, having meals prepared for them, being looked after or gaining sympathy. These things can be a real driver to keep the old behaviour rather than change – why would they want to give them up?

So, when you are going to make changes to something that has significant secondary gain, you need to understand the positive intention of the secondary gain too and ensure that what it gives you is met in a new way. You can use the 'chunking' process we mentioned earlier in the chapter to discover something else you could do that would ensure that the needs of the secondary gain are met.

So, before you make any changes, think about the consequences and ecology of the change as without this there could be the possibility of the change not sticking!

Key Learnings

The key learnings from this chapter are:

1. NLP presuppositions are the principles that successful people live by.
2. Living 'at cause' - seeks solutions and takes accountability and responsibility which leads to success.
3. Living 'at effect' - gives away your power and can lead to feeling overwhelmed, stressed and anxious.
4. Positive Intention - find out the higher-level need that the original behaviour is serving.
5. Ecology - what are the consequences of making the change? Consider these before you make any changes and manage any unintended consequences.
6. Secondary gain - what does that unwanted behaviour give you that is a benefit for you and that you will miss when you no longer do your unwanted behaviour?
7. Identify the higher positive intention of the secondary gain and find a way to meet those needs elsewhere.

CHAPTER 4 – WHAT DO YOU BELIEVE?

I mentioned beliefs briefly in Chapter 2 when we were looking at the NLP Communication Model and how 'generalisations' are another name for beliefs. In this chapter, we are going to dig a bit deeper and explore why it is so important that we understand what beliefs are and how we can change them.

Firstly, beliefs can have a big impact on motivation. If you have a belief that you are not good enough, for example, that could stop you from even trying something new.

Beliefs that are unhelpful to you in terms of your life or what you want to achieve are called 'limiting beliefs'. These can stop you from moving forward and you may even miss opportunities that are right in front of you. Beliefs create blinkers on life and a lens through which you see the world. It can make your life a lot more difficult if you have these limiting beliefs.

A belief is something which is true to you. Some beliefs are so strong and intrinsic to us that we may not even realise we have them. These beliefs tend to be emotionless as we just think they are absolutely true – a fact of life.

We create these fundamental beliefs by downloading them, when we are really young, from those around us such as our parents and teachers or the media. We learn about what's right, what's wrong, how the world should operate, how we should operate in the world and we form beliefs about who we are and how we contribute to this world. Some of these beliefs are created over time through repetition whereas others can be created by a significant emotional event or even a trauma. From these events, we decide whether the world is a good or bad place, whether we are good enough ... the list goes on. These beliefs are personal to each individual – some are helpful and others are less so. For example, I had a client who forgot their lines in a school assembly when they were young and then believed for the rest of their life (until they changed the belief with NLP, that is) that they weren't good at public speaking. They were still looking at themselves through their childhood eyes, even though this belief was 30 years out of date!

For this reason, it's very important that we are careful of the language we use around young children. Rather than saying 'you are naughty', (which speaks to them at an identity level: in other words, who they are), say 'what you have done is naughty' (which speaks to them at a behavioural level: in other words, what they have done is naughty). It is much easier to change a behaviour (which could be just a one off) than to change who you are when you have been labelled at an identity and belief level.

As you know from the last chapter on presuppositions, we are not our behaviours. This applies to children too. Although their behaviour might be less than ideal, it is the behaviour that is the problem and not the child themselves. Remember that every behaviour is motivated by a positive intention and is there to meet a fundamental need. Supporting the child to help them discover what they really need will be far more effective than labelling them with a limiting belief.

As mentioned before, after the age of 7, we delete and distort information to keep the fundamental beliefs we have already formed alive. In other words, these have become your core beliefs and you collect evidence to support those beliefs for the rest of your life. However, once you have an opportunity (such as today) to discover what you are doing, you can learn how to change those old limiting beliefs to more empowering beliefs, so that they don't hold you back anymore and you can move forward to have the life that you desire.

Some beliefs can be empowering and useful – those are the ones we like to keep. Those useful beliefs enable us to look at life through a positive lens; those that are less useful have the same lens effect but lead to a less positive outcome. When you created these beliefs, you were young and your perspective on life lacked the wisdom of experience and age because it was based on the interpretation of a child. To then continue to live your life according to this belief and see the world through this distorted lens can be less than helpful to your adult life and can sometimes feel like a child is running the show! You may even have misinterpreted someone else's actions as a child and then lived by that misinterpretation for the rest of your life. Perhaps the person that you downloaded that belief from was just feeling unresourceful and was having a bad day – this one incident doesn't need to impact your future.

It is the beliefs that aren't so useful that will be the subject of this chapter. These are the ones you may want to change.

How do you know if you have a limiting belief? Well, one of the ways to find out is to eavesdrop on yourself! Listen to your internal dialogue (known in NLP as auditory digital). What are you saying? Is it a kind, supportive and helpful voice or is it more a critical voice that is holding you back? Another way is to listen to what you say about yourself when you are talking, as this is where these beliefs can 'pop' out. Do any of these seem familiar?

- 'I can't'
- 'That's not possible for me'
- 'It's okay for everyone else but not for me'
- 'I always make a mess'
- 'I am rubbish at sport'
- 'I can never do it'
- 'I should be more organised'.

We all live our lives as a representation of our beliefs – what you have right now is a reflection of what you believe about yourself and life.

If, for example, a person believes they are not good enough, then this would be reflected in all areas of their life – maybe they don't go for a promotion because they feel they aren't good at their job. They may even find they self-sabotage, when they do go for the new job, because that old belief kicks in.

Beliefs are truly powerful things. Take placebos (tablets with no medical properties), for example. The BBC did a documentary on the placebo effect recently, which demonstrates the power of beliefs. They gathered a large group of people, who were suffering from pain. They told them that half of the group were to be given a new drug that would help with pain and the other half would be given a placebo but they were not told which group they were in. They had to take the tablets regularly and then came back after a length of time to share their discoveries. Then there was the big reveal. A proportion of the group said that they had found the tablets had worked and they had experienced significant pain relief. The thing was, all of them had been given the placebo and nobody had been given a proper drug! Some of them believed so much in the placebo that they continued to take them, even after they knew it didn't have any medically proven healing properties. This is how powerful our beliefs are – they create our reality.

Most of the time we don't even realise that we have beliefs - whether limiting or not – as they reside in our unconscious mind. Let's remind ourselves about the conscious and the unconscious mind. The conscious mind is the part we talked about in the NLP Communication Model. It can process 7 + or - 2 chunks of information at any one time. It tends to be logical and sequential as this is where thinking occurs.

Our unconscious mind is where we have the storehouse of wisdom. It processes over two million pieces of information at any one time. It's where we store all our memories and is the blueprint of our health. It simultaneously processes information and is running multiple functions all at the same time, such as remembering to breathe, to grow and to pump your blood around your body. It's expansive. This is where our potential sits.

To demonstrate this, take a moment to think about your left foot and then your right foot. Were you thinking about your left foot before I asked you to think about it? I am guessing you weren't aware of it. Your left foot was there before you thought about it and was still there after you thought about it - you just weren't consciously aware of it. So, what just happened was an exchange of information between our conscious and unconscious mind.

Our beliefs are stored in our unconscious mind and as we have discovered, some of these are out of date and are no longer relevant. They may have been relevant or even true at that point in time but are no longer true, helpful or relevant now. You grow out of some beliefs such as no longer believing in Santa but some of the deeper, more core beliefs haven't gone through that upgrade process! The great news is that you can use NLP to grow up the beliefs and change those that aren't useful to you. We can become in rapport with our unconscious mind. We can learn everything there is to learn about the old belief so we can release ourselves from it and change it.

Beliefs can also be universal rather than just personal. In other words, a large proportion of people believe them. For example, once it was thought that it was impossible to run a mile in under 4 minutes as it was thought that our human body was physically unable to do this ... that was until Roger Bannister beat the 4-minute mile. Within a couple of months, others had achieved the same thing. Had Bannister held onto that universal belief, maybe he wouldn't have achieved that goal.

Beliefs are always evolving. I'm sure if you asked people in the early 1800's, they wouldn't have imagined it possible to fly to another country. If you asked somebody in the 1940's, they wouldn't have thought it was possible to travel to the moon. There are always new innovations, learning and discoveries, which lead us to develop new beliefs. Having the flexibility to change those beliefs that aren't serving you to more empowering ones will enable you to create a more fulfilled and meaningful life and become the catalyst for innovation and creativity.

An example of a personal strong belief, which impacted on the way a person saw the world, was a case cited by Abraham Maslow. He had a client visit him who believed he was a corpse. As you read this, keep in mind this was last century! Maslow asked him, 'Does a corpse bleed?' to which the client replied, 'No, a corpse doesn't bleed'. Maslow then pricked the man with a needle and he bled. The man looked astonished and turned to him and said, 'I was wrong. A corpse does bleed!' His belief was so strong that he distorted the evidence to keep his belief alive.

Many years ago, people believed that the world was flat. We now look at that belief and think it is ridiculous but that's because our world and our lives have evolved so much since then. As you can see, beliefs can soon become outdated. Rather than living our lives with outdated beliefs, we can upgrade our beliefs to something more useful. By getting rid of those limiting beliefs, we can move from being stuck to a more empowering way of thinking and living.

I watched a YouTube video of Derren Brown recently where he was demonstrating the power of beliefs. He sent one of his team into a community to spread the rumour that a statue of a dog in their town was lucky. To cut a long story short, those who believed it was lucky found themselves being lucky. Those who didn't believe they were lucky missed the opportunities that Derren Brown had deliberately created. Derren Brown even put money on the ground in front of one man and he didn't even notice! He also gave the same man a scratch card, which could have won him a new TV, but the man chucked it in the bin! It isn't really whether people are lucky or not; it is what they believe about themselves and their situations which has the impact on whether they can even spot the opportunities in the first place, let alone decide whether or not to take them. This is how our beliefs can become self-fulfilling prophecies.

Once you have identified the limiting beliefs you want to change, you then need to think about an alternative belief that you want to have instead. It may be the opposite of what you currently believe. For example, you might decide to change a belief that you are not good enough to a belief that you are good enough just as you are.

When you're making any change in terms of beliefs, you need to make sure that you do an ecology check and consider the consequences of the change. You might believe that you cannot swim, for example. It would be foolish to simply believe that you can swim and jump straight into the water because the consequences of this could be dangerous. It would be far more sensible to change the belief to 'I can learn to swim.' You should always consider the consequences of each and every change before you make it.

Activity - how to change limiting beliefs

The process we are going to use helps you to go back to the very first time when you (unconsciously) created that limiting belief. We are going to do this using something called a timeline. We all have timelines. They are a metaphor for how we mentally store time. In other words, we store our memories of yesterday in a different way to our thoughts about tomorrow ... otherwise we wouldn't know that yesterday was yesterday, and tomorrow is tomorrow!

1. Close your eyes and think about something you did last year. When you think about that, get a sense of whereabouts in relation to you this memory is. You may find this in front of you, to the side of you, above you, below you, behind you; there's no right or wrong to this.

2. Now think about something you're going to do next year. Again, close your eyes and notice the location of those thoughts that you are creating in relation to you. Are they in front of you? To your left or right side? Or behind you? Or somewhere else? Again, there's no right or wrong answer; it's just being able to experience where you are storing those thoughts.

3. In the same way, notice where you perceive the present (the here and now).

4. Now you have these three locations – your past, present and future – notice how you can join them up by creating a line that stretches from the past, through now and into the future. This is what we call your timeline.

Now you have located your own personal timeline, you can use it to make change.

We're going to use it to go back to the very first time when you made the unconscious decision to have that limiting belief which you now want to change. Even if you don't know consciously when you made it, your unconscious mind knows. By going back to the first time you made that decision, you can revisit the situation with your adult eyes and learn all there is to learn from the situation – all those positive learnings which will enable you to let go and change your old limiting belief.

5. Before you do this, however, check the ecology. Is it ok in all areas of your life for you to make this change today? What will be the consequences?

6. When you are ready, close your eyes again.

7. Float up above the timeline you have just identified so that it is way down below. You can see the past going off in one direction and your future stretching out in another.

8. Then, by trusting your unconscious mind, you can float back along your timeline to the very first time that unwanted belief was created. You may remember a specific event or you may just get a sense when you get there. Make sure (in your imagination) that you are way above your timeline and it's far down below you. You may even want to imagine yourself in a clear bubble where you are totally safe.

9. Once above the very first event, you can look down at it way down below you and you can ask your unconscious mind what positive learnings you need to learn from this event which will enable you to let go of the unwanted emotion and the belief. This is a great opportunity to look down with your adult eyes and to look back at your younger self with the wisdom of hindsight. By looking down through your adult eyes at the child below (which is

you at the younger age), you can observe what happened to you when you created this belief and gather all those learnings, everything you need to learn from it, to enable you to move on.

10. When you think that you've got all those learnings just double check by asking, 'Is there anything else I need to learn that will enable me to resolve this original root cause situation?'

11. You can also ask, 'What advice would I give my younger self in relation to this, which will enable me to be free from this limiting belief?'

Some of your learnings might be similar to these:
- you were only a child
- the expectations were unreasonable
- it didn't really matter in the bigger scheme of things
- you had misunderstood this situation.

There can be many learnings which will be unique to you. Make sure the learnings are positive as you will take them forward with you into your future, so that you can let go of the unwanted belief and emotion around the first event.

12. Once you have gathered all those learnings, you can reassure your unconscious mind that you can store all those learnings in a safe place, should you ever need them. The highest positive intention of your unconscious mind is protection, so it will only allow you to let go when it feels safe. With all those positive learnings having been stored away safely – there for you whenever you need them – you can now float into the event.

13. Notice how different this feels. If there are still emotions or a limiting belief, then you can float back up and check what else you need to learn.

14. Repeat going into the event again and notice if this has

now changed. You can even give love and advice to the younger you in that situation in your imagination, so that you can enable your younger you to be supported.

15. Once it feels different, just check – what do you believe now? Is it different?

16. Once you are ready, you can float back up above the event and along your timeline back to now, noticing how all those events along your timeline are changed in light of your learnings and your new belief. You can notice the ripples of success along your timeline as that new belief impacts on all of your life.

17. When you get to the present day, you can take the new belief and float out into the future to a specific situation where, if it had happened in the past, you would have had that old belief, and notice what you believe now instead.

18. Float to a second event in the future, where if it had happened in the past, you would have had that old belief, and notice how different it is now.

19. Go to a third event, even further out in the future. Notice how different that looks and experience your amazing, incredible new belief. Once you have done that, float back to now and then back into the room and ask yourself, 'So what do I believe now?' Notice how different that feels.

You may find it easier to record yourself reading this or you can just open your eyes, read what you have to do next and then close your eyes and complete the next step. Either works well. Alternatively, find an NLP professional to help guide you through.

So, how do you apply this in terms of your life? I suggest you start from where you are right now. Spend a moment being quiet and listening to that internal dialogue and noticing what beliefs may be coming up for you.

You can use this technique to change those beliefs – from small beliefs through to significant beliefs. Remember some of those beliefs have been there for a while and you may just think they are the truth. If that's the case, just remember the stories of the 'truths' we had around the world being flat and about being able to run a mile in under 4 minutes.

You can use this tool on a regular basis - when you're listening to yourself, when you're chatting to friends or when you're just about to do a new activity. Notice what comes into your mind. If you find that it's an unwanted negative belief about yourself, use this technique to make change. If you're finding yourself saying things about yourself to yourself that you would never say to a friend, then that's also a good indication of a limiting belief. It's worth spending time on this because this can give you a whole new perspective on life. Think of those things you've never tried to do because you thought you weren't good enough or you weren't worthy and those things you thought were only available for somebody else. You can change your beliefs to enable you to do these things.

This is where you may discover layers. When you uncover one set of limiting beliefs, you may find other ones pop up. It's a journey, not a quick fix. By using this and the other tools that you're going to learn in this book, you'll be able to move forward, so you can start to have that life you truly desire; the one that's free from those things that are holding you back and includes the new and exciting opportunities that you can create by removing those unwanted beliefs.

You may also discover that by changing a higher level belief, there is a ripple effect on other beliefs. For example, by changing a belief around not being able to learn new things, you may discover that you can learn the new computer system at work, how to cook, how to do a new hobby – the list goes on.

By asking the question, 'What would you do if you couldn't fail?' you will get a good indication of any remaining limiting beliefs that are holding you back. If you become aware of any 'yes, buts ...' popping up, these too are indications of limiting beliefs and you know you can now clear them if you want to (remembering to do your ecology check first, of course). This will open up a whole new world of possibilities and opportunities for you as you expand your map of the world and discover a more fulfilling and meaningful life where you can unleash your true potential.

Key Learnings

The key learnings from this chapter are:

1. Your core beliefs were downloaded from other people by the age of 7.
2. After the age of 7, we delete and distort information to protect those beliefs.
3. Beliefs are truisms for you; the things that you believe are true from your map of the world.
4. Beliefs are the fundamental foundations upon which your map of the world was created.
5. Beliefs that aren't working for you are called limiting beliefs and you can change them.
6. Beliefs can be so strong that they can stop you even trying something new.
7. Beliefs can also inhibit motivation and become self-fulfilling prophecies as we delete and distort information and gather evidence to keep those beliefs alive.
8. Many of our limiting beliefs are out of date because they were created when we were young and are no longer relevant.
9. You can change these limiting beliefs by using your timeline and gathering your learnings from the original event.
10. You can tell if you have a limiting belief by listening to your own language, for example, I can't ..., I always ..., I should ..., I have to ..., yes, but ...
11. New empowering beliefs tend to be the opposite of the original limiting beliefs.

CHAPTER 5 – INTERPRETATION DRIVES YOUR RESPONSE

As we saw with the NLP Communication Model, once the information has gone through our filters of deletion, distortion and generalisation, we then get to the internal representation part of the model. We touched on it briefly as the 'movie in your mind' and now we are going to investigate it in a bit more detail. It is our internal representation of an event that we use to generate meaning, such as whether something is good or bad. This in turn impacts on how we interpret this information, which subsequently dictates how we feel about the event.

Take the word 'Christmas', for example.

Notice what springs to mind when you see that word. What is your interpretation? Is it one of joy and time with the family? Or is it one of frustration, sadness, busyness or loneliness? Or something else? This is based on your own past experience and memories. Your filters have created a lens through which you interpret meaning from just this one word.

So, you can see that one word, such as 'Christmas', can have multiple interpretations and in fact fires off a set of neurological connections within your mind.

Activity – eliciting submodalities

1. Think of an event that happened recently – a good event, one that you enjoyed. It can be anything – a nice walk in the countryside, a lovely meal – anything.

2. Close your eyes and think about that event.

3. Notice what images, sounds or feelings are generated from thinking about this event.

4. Note down the answers to the following questions:

- Are there any pictures that are important? If so, are they in black and white or in colour?
- Are they moving or are they still?
- Are there multiple pictures or just one?
- Is the picture in focus or is it blurry?
- Is the focus changing?
- Is there a frame around the picture or is it panoramic?
- Where is the picture located? Is it near you or far away? Is it above you or below you?
- Are you in the picture and looking at yourself or are you looking through your own eyes?

5. Now notice whether there are any sounds that are important around the event.
   - What's the volume of the sounds?
   - Are they loud or quiet?
   - Are they muffled?
   - What about the tone? Is it pleasing or grating?
   - What direction are the sounds coming from?
   - Are they internal or external sounds?

6. Then notice whether there are any feelings that are important around the event.
   - Where are those feelings located?
   - Are they inside or outside your body?
   - How intense are they?
   - Do they have a shape to them or movement?

This is probably the first time you've actually thought about an event in this way as we don't consciously register that level of detail. This is important because the way you've stored the memory of the event will impact on the meaning you will apply to it. By knowing this, you can make changes.

7. Now think about another event - one that maybe didn't go so well or that you didn't enjoy so much. Close your eyes and as you think about the event, ask yourself the same questions. Remember to write down your observations.

8. Compare the two lists. The chances are they will be different. This is how we know the difference between something we like and something we dislike. If those images, sounds and feelings were exactly the same, located in the same place and had the same details, it is highly likely we would feel the same way about the two events. We call these details submodalities as they are the qualities and details of our modalities or senses (what we see, hear, feel, smell and taste).

You will store something you like in a different location and in a different way to something you dislike. For example, say you hate cabbage – your interpretation of cabbage would be stored in a different place or in a different way to where you store your interpretation of something you love such as ice-cream.

It is these qualities or details that enable us to recognise the difference between something we enjoy and something we don't enjoy or something we believe in and something we don't believe in. We store our memories using these submodalities, which create a unique metaphorical filing system within our brains for events, information and beliefs, enabling us to make sense of the world.

This is important because sometimes we store things in our unconscious mind in a way that is less than helpful for us. For example, we might dislike vegetables but this may be less than helpful because vegetables are good for us. We might want to learn to like vegetables. We can do this by changing how we store our perception of vegetables in our unconscious mind. We can move the image, sounds and feelings to a place where we store the things we like. This is great news because it means that we don't have to be stuck with decisions we made years ago!

You can change all kinds of things which aren't working for you – from something small such as a dislike of maths, right through to bigger things such as what you believe about yourself. You can even gain clarity over something you are 'confused' about, by moving it to the place where you store the things that are 'clear' to you. I love the analogy of our minds being like a huge office with various filing cabinets. You can start to move around the files in the filing cabinets of your mind.

If you would like to, you can use the exercise you did at the beginning of the chapter to make a change. You can change the image, sounds or feelings of the event you didn't enjoy so much to the submodalities of the one that you did enjoy. As always, remember to check the ecology first though – is it ok to make this change in every area of your life? What will be the consequences?

To make the change, look down the list of answers you have for each event and notice the differences. For simplicity, I'll illustrate this by changing just one submodality. Let's imagine that the memory you did not enjoy was in black and white but the memory you did enjoy was in colour.

Follow these steps:
- Close your eyes and picture the original image of the memory you did not enjoy (which was black and white).
- Keeping the picture otherwise the same, simply change the picture in your mind to colour.
- Now, one by one, change all the other submodalities (image, sound and feelings), so that the memory you did not enjoy has now taken on all the submodalities of the memory you did enjoy.

Notice how different that event is now when you think about it.

Changing how you store your internal images has an impact on how you feel and therefore how you behave. Have you ever been to a business meeting and found it boring and then dreaded the next meeting? This is because you created an internal representation in your mind of the meeting being boring, which then becomes a self-fulfilling prophecy. However, when you change the submodalities of the meeting, you will have a different perspective or lens through which to view the next meeting.

We have a particular part of our brain called the Reticular

Activating System or RAS for short. This is the part of the brain that helps us to get what we are focusing on. If, for example, you have ever bought a new car, you may have noticed as soon as you are on the road that every other car seems to be the same as yours. Or maybe you have noticed when you got a new pet that everything you see or read seems to be about pets ... well, that is your RAS at work.

Our RAS also comes into play (but in a less helpful way) when we have an existing (negative) internal representation of an event or person. Even when we haven't experienced something exactly like it, our brains will find a similar or equivalent experience in order to make sense of what is happening and to generate meaning. Our filters of distortion, deletion and generalisation come into play more than once – first when we filter the information initially (during the live experience) and again each time we recall the event or person. Therefore, if you have an unhelpful internal representation around a particular event or person, your RAS will be looking for the same thing to happen again the second time you meet them or experience that event and each subsequent time. By changing the submodalities, this can enable a different experience.

Activity – changing submodalities

1. Think about something you find less than easy.

2. Close your eyes and notice the pictures, sounds or feelings you have of it.

3. Change the submodalities: add colour, move the location, change the tonality of the sounds, the intensity of the feelings until the memory feels better in your mind. Make any changes necessary to enhance the picture, sounds or feelings and notice the difference next time you do that thing.

Remember the equation: Event + Response = Outcome

By changing the submodalities, we are changing our internal

representation of the event, which will in turn have an impact on our response as it gives us greater choice over our behaviour and emotions which will subsequently impact our outcome.

We can start to use this changing of the movie in our mind to enable better outcomes for us in advance. For example, imagine that you have a presentation coming up at work and when you think about it, you have less than helpful images, sounds or feelings. By changing this internal representation of the presentation to something that feels more positive, or looks better or sounds more encouraging, this will help you to enable your RAS (Reticular Activating System) to start to look for a more positive experience during the preparation as well as during the delivery of the presentation. Life events happen ... what we are doing is making them more pleasurable for us.

There is a great movie called *About Time*. I won't spoil it for you if you haven't seen it. The part that stuck with me was when one of the characters was able to replay a day over and over and could make changes each time to make it better. He would have his normal day with all the stresses, anxieties and issues that life threw at him. He would then go through the day again. This time he appreciated all the good things – he thanked the shop assistant, he looked for the positives and he celebrated his successes. After a while, he didn't need to live the day over ... he lived it to the full each and every day, which is a great lesson for all of us. With this tool, you can start to make this a reality for you and in effect have an upgrade on your internal representation – making it into a HD movie rather than a silent black and white one! Your life will become a richer experience.

Some people who struggle in terms of self-esteem compare themselves with others. They focus on what they believe others are thinking of them or how they are being judged. The reality is that most people are more worried about themselves and how they are coming across! So, start to change your movie in your mind to have a different interpretation – this is within your remit to do.

After all, we all have our own unique version of our model of the world and therefore we are normally judging what is happening based on our own internal bias rather than facts. In other words, we are 'mindreading' what is going on with other people based on our version of reality. We are filling in the gaps of information using our own unique bias rather than just interpreting the facts as they stand. We all have this unconscious bias going on. The bottom line is that we are 'making things up' – even if we are not doing it consciously. We think we know what is going on in another person's world, even if we really have no idea. We do it so that we can make sense of the world and other people. We don't, however, know whether our interpretation is true or not. Therefore, if you are going to make something up, you may as well make up something positive!

So, if your interpretation of a person's behaviour is unhelpful, upgrade your movie to create a different outcome. Focus on the good in others, in the situation, (the opportunities rather than the problems) and this will give you greater choice, open up possibilities and ultimately generate a better outcome for you.

Let me give you an example. My friend had started a new job and after a couple of weeks, her new colleague became quiet and stopped speaking to her. My friend thought that she had done something wrong and this upset and worried her for days. She had 'mind-read' the situation; filled in the gaps of the information with her own interpretation – her 'made-up' analysis of the situation. It turned out there were other events happening in this woman's home life that had really upset her and it was nothing to do with work. This is the kind of situation I am talking about. We so often interpret situations through mind-reading and act as if it is truth, without actually finding out what is really happening.

In the example just given, my friend could have saved herself days of heartache. So, if you find yourself mindreading, you have two options:
- Ask questions to find out what is actually going on for the other person (we talk about how to ask great questions later in the language section)

- Reframe the situation to help you to think about it in a slightly different way.

Reframing

Reframing is the art of thinking differently. It is really useful when you want a different interpretation of a situation, to create a better outcome for yourself.

We are going to look at two types of reframing: context and content. Both are lenses through which we can see life.

As you know, we are interpreting situations all the time based on our own version of reality, our own personal unconscious biases, our filters ... to such an extent that we may not even realise that they are in operation. This technique will enable us to have a more helpful interpretation. After all, if you are upset about something, the other person may not even have realised what has happened for you to feel that way. If (for whatever reason) you can't ask them about it, you can reframe it.

(i)   Content reframe

This is where you ask yourself, 'what else could this behaviour mean?'

Let's take an example. A couple of years ago I had arranged to meet my husband shopping in town at a certain time, in a certain shop. I arrived in plenty of time and waited and waited and waited! I called him but he didn't answer his phone. What would you have thought? A number of scenarios went through my mind. Did he forget? Had something happened to him? I didn't know what was happening and I realised that I was mind-reading. As I couldn't ask him at that point, I deliberately chose what to think so that I stayed in a resourceful state. In other words, I reframed the meaning around him being late from him being rude to something more helpful. I reframed it that maybe he had met a friend or got held up at work, so I felt calm and resourceful when he did turn up, rather than annoyed.

After a good while, he did turn up – covered in grease! He had helped someone who had a puncture to change their wheel. I was so grateful that I had reframed the situation, rather than becoming angry.

Sometimes you have the opportunity to discover what really happened (like in my example above) and sometimes you will never know (like if somebody cuts you up at a junction). In both these cases, being able to reframe to something more useful for us is really helpful in terms of our own emotional and mental well-being. In addition, this impacts how we behave in response to the situation and therefore on our outcome.

Reframing the 'content' (the meaning of the situation) gives us greater choice. Take the example of somebody cutting you up at a junction – maybe that person was in a rush, maybe they didn't see you, maybe they were distracted at that moment, maybe they weren't feeling well, maybe they were rushing to hospital ... all of these things are viable options and again we are no more certain that these are correct than our original assumption. However, when we see the situation through these lenses – this reframe – then this could change how we behave and feel about the situation. If we think the person was being rude, we may feel upset and get cross. However, if we think the person might be rushing to hospital to see a sick loved one, we are more likely to feel compassion. The outcome for us will be different as the emotion connected with the event will be different. So, as I've said before, if you are going to make something up, you may as well make up something positive as this will have a more positive outcome for you.

In the example of my friend, you can see that her interpretation of her work colleague's behaviour was just a mind-read with no evidence of truth. So, to make up something different such as 'it is nothing to do with me,' or 'maybe she has some other issues going on' would have given her days of calm rather than anguish. If we don't have the opportunity to actually ask the other person what is going on, then we can reframe the meaning (content) so that the outcome for us is better.

(ii)   Context reframe

Another type of reframing is 'context' reframe. This is where the behaviour is appropriate in one situation whereas it is less appropriate in another. A person who displays argumentative behaviour can be less than easy in a friendly conversation over dinner, however, they could be very useful in a court of law or a debating society. When you change the context and find a time when that behaviour would be useful, this can help you to change the label from being a 'bad' behaviour' to one which, in a different context, could be useful. Take, for example, the tenacity that young people have to play on the X Box – some can label this a waste of time, but this tenacity can serve them well in their future careers. There was an advert recently by The Armed Forces stating that this is what they are looking for – those who have the tenacity and strategy to succeed. This shift of perspective can, therefore, give us a new-found and more tolerant approach to life and others' actions.

Using both context and content reframing can widen our map of the world and stretch our current perspective so that we can have better outcomes and a richer and fuller life. For example, take that person who appears to only ever contact you when they want something ... maybe they are not just 'using you'; maybe you are the person that they can rely on and trust to be a true friend in times of need (content reframe). That person who is being really quiet in a meeting may not be disinterested ... maybe they are just shy. How you treat them could be different dependent on how you have mind-read their behaviour. This will impact on your relationship with the other person.

Remember, people are not usually trying to deliberately upset or irritate you! With this reframing tool, you can change your interpretation and meaning so that you react in a different way. They will no longer get the reaction they expect and you move from feeling like a victim to being in control of your life, which is super empowering. You have choice over your reactions and can focus on how you want to be, rather than feeling at the mercy of others. We will add to this subject later in the book when we talk about communication, relationships and the language to use to enable us to have better relationships with others and have a more empowering and positive perspective on life.

Key Learnings

The key learnings from this chapter are:

1. RAS (Reticular Activating System) enables you to get what you focus on.
2. We create an internal representation (movie in our mind) of events and situations which are unique to us and through which we generate meaning.
3. We can change these internal representations, if they are not working for us, to create different outcomes, to have better relationships with others and to make changes.
4. We mind-read actions all the time – creating an interpretation which may or may not be correct, based on our map of the world.
5. We can change that interpretation by reframing – looking at the behaviour/meaning from a different perspective or a different context where it would be useful.
6. By changing our interpretation and meaning, we can change our response and therefore the outcome to even the most challenging situations.

CHAPTER 6 – HOW TO MANAGE YOUR EMOTIONS

Emotions are a huge subject and NLP has a lot to say about them! Here we are going to talk about some of the key emotions that we may experience through life, the reason we feel some of these emotions as we go through change and how to feel differently, especially if we are feeling stuck.

The first thing that is important to remember is that emotions are a natural and normal part of life – this is what makes us human, after all!

In NLP we avoid labelling emotions as 'good' or 'bad' – instead, we like to look at whether they are useful in the given situation. When they are useful, we look at how we can enhance them to make them even more useful. If they are less than helpful, we look at how we can change them, so we can feel something more empowering.

Different situations warrant different emotions. If someone is in an unhealthy relationship, they may feel angry and this could be the driver for them to leave. However, if they always felt calm, maybe they would stay in that unhealthy relationship. As you can see, anger in this instance is useful – it could be a catalyst for change. However, if they kept on being angry and taking that emotion forward into new relationships, this could be less than helpful for them and something they may want to change.

Maybe you feel frustrated with a client or work colleague to the point that it gets in the way of you expressing your point of view. This can be less than helpful. If you felt more resourceful, you would be able to communicate more clearly.

We can't necessarily change the situation but we can change how we feel about it.

If you go through significant change, for example, it is likely that you will experience a number of different emotions. In the 1960s, Kubler Ross developed The Change Curve to explain the grieving process. This curve has since been extensively used in business as well as to explain what happens when an individual goes through significant change. The emotions include: shock, denial, anger, depression and acceptance. It is normal and natural to go through all of these emotions at some stage and they won't necessarily be in that order! You may find yourself moving throughout these emotions at different times, doubling back or staying in one place longer than others. NLP can help if you find yourself stuck in any of these emotions or you want to move through the curve more easily.

As mentioned in Chapter 3, we always look at the ecology of doing any change work. What will the consequences be? What will we gain or lose? Remember when looking at the ecology of decisions, we are not necessarily saying we don't want change – we are just making sure that the results will be what we want.

Say you felt angry, for example. What would happen when you changed it? You would be calmer. It might lower your blood pressure. Relationships could become easier. And what might you lose? A sense of control? In NLP, we want to make sure that the positive intention of any change is maintained. If the positive intention was a sense of control, you could still maintain this sense of control by calmly and resourcefully solving the problem, rather than getting angry. That way you would still have the positive intention and have a better outcome

The physical impact of our emotions

From a physical perspective, some emotions are more helpful than others. Psychoneuroimmunology is a field of research which discovered that our thoughts and emotions have a physical impact on our bodies. Scientists found that when we are angry, cortisol and adrenalin (bio-chemicals) are pumped around our bodies, raising our heart rate and blood pressure. This is known as the stress response and triggers our fight/flight stimulus.

These chemicals are necessary when we are in a situation which calls for us to have such a response (to run away, fight or freeze in a dangerous situation). However, in the majority of our lives, we are not in these life or death situations. If we are stressed or angry because the train is late, for example, these chemicals are still being produced even though we don't actually need them. So, what happens to them? Well, they are pumped around our bodies for up to 24 hours following the incident, raising our blood pressure and heart rate until we finally calm down. The trouble is, this isn't very good for us physically and has an impact on our immune system if we continue this pattern over time.

Advances in neuroscience have demonstrated that what we think and focus on has an impact on our physical body and health – in particular, our immune system (psychoneuroimmunology). It looks at three elements – psychological, neurological and immunological (Cain et al, 2005). The three elements are linked to what we are thinking. If we are stressed and having unhelpful thoughts, this will impact on our physiology (how we physically feel) as we will be sending those less than helpful bio-chemicals around our bodies, which impacts on our immune system.

If, however, we are thinking positive thoughts and more positive neurological networks are firing in our brains, then the unwanted bio-chemicals aren't sent around our system and therefore don't have the negative impact on our immune system.

More recent research has demonstrated that stress can increase the spread of cancer and other stress-related illnesses such as psoriasis.

What can we do about it?

We can start to change this pattern. There are a number of brilliant NLP techniques to help you do this. I recommend working with a certified NLP professional to explore these.

In this chapter, we are going to explore a couple of these techniques that you can use yourself to start to make these changes.

The NLP Model we are going to talk about is called the Mercedes Model because it looks like a Mercedes car badge! The principle is that when you change one of the three elements, you will start to experience a change in state (how you feel).

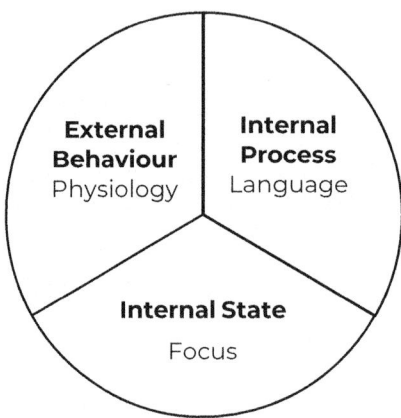

The Internal State (focus)

The first element is the internal state (how we are feeling, which is impacted by what we are focusing on). When you change what you focus on, you will change how you feel. Therefore, when you focus on what you have, rather than what you don't have, you will start to feel more grateful.

You may have heard the term 'where attention goes, energy flows.' Well, your RAS (Reticular Activating System), as covered in the last chapter, helps with focusing our attention and will enable your energy to be aligned.

This is akin to the well know phrase 'you get what you focus on'. If your focus is on negativity and looking for all the things that aren't going well, that is what you will find. On the other hand, when you start to focus on all the things that are going well and all the things that you have and are grateful for, your RAS will find you more of this. As Henry Ford said, 'Whether you think you can or think you can't, you are right'. This is why it is so important to train your RAS so that you can start to focus on what you can control and what you want rather than what you can't control and what you don't want.

How do you do that? Well firstly, let's explore this idea of focusing on what we can control rather than what we can't. If we constantly focus on what we can't control, we can start to feel helpless, hopeless and stressed. As I'm sure you know, a little bit of stress isn't harmful but it is a different story when the brain has a long period of chronic stress (see *Seven and a Half Lessons about the Brain* by Lisa Feldman Barrett). This regular feeling of overwhelm and lack of control is something that would be good to change.

If you constantly focus on the problem, this is what your RAS will find you – more problems. If, however, you focus on what you can control – the solution to your problem (even if it is little things like what you wear or what you eat) – then this will start to help you to feel more in control and you can get back into the pilot's seat of your life.

A lovely question I use when training is this: who is flying your plane? Is it you? Or are you letting someone or something else dictate what happens in your life? Clearly there are rules that we all need to live by, but we can focus on what is within our remit to change and remember we can always choose our response and emotions. Life seems a whole lot easier when we are feeling resourceful enough to steer our own plane.

When you are ready, you can start to take this to the next level. Start to get your RAS to focus on amazing things for you – abundance, joy and hope. Meditation is a great way to help us refocus our RAS. I love the *21 Days of Abundance* meditation by Deepak Chopra. I remember one morning after doing the meditation, I went to get the post and we had received 5 envelopes – all of them telling us about money coming into our lives.

What do you want your RAS to focus on? If you are going into a meeting and you are focusing on it being boring, the chances are your RAS will find 'boring'. If, however, you ask your RAS to focus on 'interesting' or 'useful', this is what you will be more likely to find.

External Behaviour (physiology)

The second element of the Mercedes Model refers to making a physical change in terms of what you are doing. You might go for a walk or a run, change posture or even do star jumps to change your state! If you are cycling or running, you are less likely to remain in your angry state, for example. Most people will see a change in how they feel by changing their physiology. Just standing up straight and taking on a positive, confident stance will change how you are feeling.

There was a piece of research in America where a cinema full of customers were split in half. One half were asked to watch the movie with a pencil in their mouths lengthwise – from corner to corner – causing them to smile. The other half had the pencil sticking out of their mouths like a straw. Afterwards they were asked to rate what they had seen. Those whose physiology was in a smile enjoyed it more than those who had the pencil as a straw! It just shows that our physiology is a powerful tool for change.

Another way to change your physiology is by changing your breathing. There is a very quick technique you can use to help you feel calmer and less stressed or less angry. Gently breathe in for a count of 4 and then breathe out for longer (you may want to breathe in for 4 and out for 6). This will slow down your heart rate and can lower your blood pressure and bring back some balance to your mood.

Internal Process (language)

The third element in the model is your internal process or your language. When you change what you are saying to yourself or others, this will change how you are feeling – it will also have an impact on your physiology and focus.

I went through a large proportion of my life not realising the power of our words – that the language we use impacts on the way we feel. Now that you understand the power of your RAS, you can start to appreciate the power of your language.

When we look at words, I like to consider them on a continuum, for example, with 'hard' at one end and 'easy' at the other. When you take one step away from 'hard' and say that it is 'less than easy', then your RAS will start to look for easy for you. Why? Well, because our minds can't process negation. Think of your mind as an internet search engine. If you type 'not a pink elephant' into the search engine, what results will you get? You will get a pink elephant rather than everything except a pink elephant! Our brains work in the same way. We need to be specific about what we want rather than what we don't want. If you wake up in the morning saying, 'I'm so tired and exhausted,' then your body will respond physically in that way. Those neurological pathways of 'tired' and 'exhausted' will be firing and the result will be that you will feel more tired and exhausted, creating a stronger neurological pathway every time you say it. However, if you say you feel 'less than energetic', your brain will process the word 'energetic' and put you on the path to energetic!

Another way to see how your language can impact on your physiology is to find a partner and ask them to hold their arm out straight in front of them (making sure that they are healthy and are injury free, of course). Pull down gently on their arm as you ask them to resist you and notice how strong they are. Then ask them to say, 'I'm strong like superman' three times over and then pull down again and see if there is a difference. Repeat the activity again and this time ask them to say, 'I'm weak and pathetic' three times and notice the difference in their physiology. If you want to see a demonstration of this, visit the Achieve Your Greatness YouTube channel.

In summary, when you change one of the three areas of the Mercedes Model – focus, language or physiology – you will change your state. When you change more than one, even better! Each has a knock-on effect. Our language impacts on our physiology, our physiology has an impact on our focus and our focus has an impact on our language and vice versa. So, making a small change in one of these areas will start to help you to see a shift in the other area and help change your outcome.

It is all about choice – how do you want to feel?

Event + Response = Outcome

Our emotional state sits in the 'response' part and is something that is under our control. This is something we do have the power to change.

From a neuroscience perspective, there is a trigger (stimulus response), which fires off a neurological connection, which gives you an emotional response. So, it is a bit like turning on a light bulb – you flick the switch and the light goes on.

The great news is that, due to neuroplasticity, existing neurological connections in terms of unwanted emotions can be changed and new ones can be created at any time. Neuroplasticity is 'the ability of the brain to develop new neurons and/or new synapses in response to stimulation and learning.' (OxfordReference.com). In essence, this is like going through a jungle with a machete for the first time. It may be less than easy as you cut your way through to create the new path (to calm, for example). The more you use it, this new path becomes easier and easier to travel through and over time, the old pathway (to anger, for example,) starts to become overgrown!

In NLP, we use neuroplasticity to create new neurological pathways. We call this 'anchoring' – deliberately creating a desired stimulus response using classic conditioning (repetition). This means you can have new neurological pathways to more resourceful emotions that you can use whenever you need them.

Anchors are all around us and we create them naturally and automatically. Think of your favourite song and notice how it makes you feel. This is an auditory anchor. You hear the song and it immediately fires off a neurological pathway in your brain of a particular state or feeling. The anchor could be visual (a photo of a loved one) or kinaesthetic (a hug). These are naturally occurring neurological connections. When we deliberately create an anchor, we are just applying the science behind these so that we can have more choice over how we want to feel and start to create some new resources for ourselves. There are also olfactory (smell) and gustatory (taste) anchors.

Activity – creating a kinaesthetic anchor

What emotions do you want more of? Learning to be able to access those states easily can be really helpful so that they are there for you when you need them.

You can create a kinaesthetic anchor. This means that with the press of your finger, you can trigger a positive emotional response whenever you want it.

1. As always, do an ecology check first. Is it okay for you to have this new emotion now and available to you in the future?

2. Then decide where you want to create this anchor. I suggest a knuckle, for example. It needs to be somewhere where you can easily (and discretely) press it when you need it.

3. Now, think about a time when you experienced the emotion you want to have more of and go back in your mind to that specific time.

    Look at the situation through your own eyes and see what you saw. Notice what you heard when you felt this emotion. How did you feel? Notice what it is like to feel those feelings right now. Notice how you stood and breathed when you felt this emotion and do that now. Say what you said to yourself when you had those feelings. Once you have started to feel those feelings, you can imagine a dial from 1 to 10 where 1 is really low and 10 is a really strong feeling. You can notice where you are on the dial at the moment and then start to turn up the dial until it is at about an 8, making those feeling stronger and stronger with every breath.

4. At that moment, press your knuckle and hold it as you ramp up the feeling to 8.5, 9 and 9.5 ... remove your finger just before your imaginary dial reaches 10.

5. Repeat steps 3 and 4 a number of times to create this new neurological pathway, which becomes stronger and stronger every time you do it. In other words, the messages that are being passed from neuron to neuron via the synaptic gate (the gap between neurons) is getting stronger and stronger every time you do it. In essence, the neurons are becoming wired together to create an automatic response.

6. Now go and do or think about something else and then press your knuckle and see how that feels. Notice how quickly those feelings come back. If you would like that feeling to be even stronger, continue to repeat the process until it is as strong as you want it to be.

You can now use this resource anchor whenever you want to feel this emotion – all you have to do is press your knuckle. In the same way as looking at and smelling your favourite food makes you feel good, firing your anchor gives you access to the state that you wanted more of. In essence, you have created a new 'stimulus response': an automatic, unconscious response from a trigger. Neuroplasticity is pretty cool stuff!

You can create different anchors on different knuckles for different emotional states - confidence, calm or patience, for example. Remember that when you create an anchor, the resource needs to be positively stated (say what you want rather than what you don't want). For example, say that you want to feel 'relaxed' or 'calm' rather than 'not stressed.' Remember our pink elephant in an internet search engine!

In the same way that emotions such as anger, stress and frustration can have a negative impact on our immune system and physiology, positive emotions such as happiness, confidence and joy can have a positive effect. There have been a number of studies where it has been found that positive emotions have had a significant impact on physical health, as well as mental health. Norman Cousin's book, *Anatomy of an Illness* is a great example - he used laughter to help cure himself of illness.

How can we reduce worry?

Let's talk about worry for a moment. Worry is a prediction or thought about something in the future, which by definition, hasn't happened yet. It can also be when we are thinking unhelpful thoughts about another person and sending negative energy their way.

As we have mentioned before, our minds are projectors, not cameras – we are therefore projecting our map of the world and making up the future which hasn't yet occurred. So, if you are worrying about something that hasn't yet happened, you are making something up and then feeling negative about it, which is less than helpful for you physically and mentally.

So, what can you do instead? Well, if you are going to make something up, I suggest you make up something useful or take action to enable things to turn out better.

Say, for example, you are worrying about an interview. There are a few things you can do that are within your influence:
- Prepare (research the company, create your portfolio, collate information about your achievements)
- Create yourself a resource anchor
- Start to visualise it going well. As you know by now, this

will ensure your RAS will look out for things to go well (you get what you focus on!) Your mind cannot differentiate between reality and something we have made up, so the more you visualise the interview going well, the more your mind will believe you have done this before! New and useful neurological pathways will be created (see Chapter 7 for more on visualisation).

If you find yourself worrying about another person, remember the living 'at cause' or living 'at effect' concepts. If we are taking on third party issues that we can't do anything about and making ourselves feel bad about it, we are living 'at effect' – we are giving away our power. You can either do something about it by engaging with and supporting the other person or you can send them positive energy. Either of these options are far better than sending them negative worry.

Dr Emoto demonstrated that human vibrations and energy, thoughts, ideas and music affect the molecular structure of water. Knowing our bodies are made up of 70% water, this is worth taking note of. You can see his work either in his book, *The Message from Water* or look at the pictures on YouTube of different water molecular structures that have been exposed to different words, music and emotions. Positive words created beautifully symmetrical crystals, whereas negative words had the opposite effect.

To be clear, I am not saying we shouldn't care for others – not at all. It is just better to do so in a constructive, helpful and empathetic way, rather than sending negative energy by worrying.

If you are going to predict the future, then rather than worry about it, decide on the outcome you want and take action. If things aren't going the way you anticipate, then be flexible and work out what you can do next. Worry uses up energy and impacts on your mental and physical well-being.

In NLP we also have something called the act 'as if' frame. This means that you act 'as if' you are already in this state. This can be really useful when it comes to states such as confidence. We can also use it when we create anchors – especially if we want to access a state that is relatively new to us or we haven't experienced before. For example, think about a person who you admire and who is super confident. How do you know they are confident? Are you sure that they are not just pretending ... acting 'as if'? Notice what happens when you act 'as if' you are as confident as them.

Hans Vaihinger completed his major philosophical work *Die Philosophie Des Als Ob (1911) (The Philosophy of 'As If'),* which suggests that man is constantly acting 'as if'. In order for us to survive, we construct fictional explanations of phenomena 'as if' there were rational grounds for believing such a method reflects reality. When we think about the NLP Communication Model, we are constantly deleting, distorting and generalising information to meet our version of reality and then acting 'as if' our version is true. So, with that in mind, if a person is nervous – how do we know this is true? Maybe they are just acting 'as if' they are nervous? Knowing that we can act 'as if' can loosen the restrictions or labels we put on ourselves. With the power of your mind, you can generate your reality by acting 'as if' you are confident and that is your truth. Vaihinger identified that every person is acting 'as if' in every moment of their life ... so if this is the case, why not act 'as if' we are confident or happy? This will have a positive impact on our mental and physical well-being.

Emotions are a huge subject and we have just touched the surface to give you some ideas and tips as to what you can do to start to make choices over how you feel and to have the states that you want more of.

Key Learnings

The key learnings from this chapter are:

1. Emotions have an impact on us physically as well as mentally.
2. We can change our emotions by changing our focus, language and/or physiology.
3. We can deliberately create a resource anchor to access useful states whenever we need to.
4. We can act 'as if' to access more of the states we desire (until they become our new normal).

CHAPTER 7 – HOW TO CHANGE BEHAVIOURS

I am sure when we think about it, we all have those habits or behaviours that we wish we didn't have – swearing, shouting, nail biting, overeating to name but a few. We do these things automatically and afterwards we may experience feelings of guilt or remorse.

If you have behaviours that you want to change, this chapter is for you.

As you know, NLP can give you the tools to make changes and to have more choice over how you behave and what you do. This can give you a better quality of life as you can create the life you truly desire, rather than one that is dictated by old habits and unhelpful behaviours.

Remember to check that you really want this outcome in every area of your life before making any changes (the ecology check).

We create habits over time – these are the things you find yourself saying or doing on a regular basis. A neurological pathway has been created in your mind. As soon as it is triggered, it sets off an automatic pattern of behaviour – just like when you knock down the first domino in a row, the rest follow automatically. Behaviours become entrenched and turn into habits because the more we do something, the more it happens automatically at an unconscious level, due to neuroplasticity (see the last chapter).

The trigger that starts this chain reaction can be something you see, hear or feel. For example, if someone cuts you up on the road (a visual trigger) and you find yourself pressing the horn without even thinking, this is one of these patterns of behaviours which we call habits.

Visualisation

In order for you to create a new outcome, you can use something called visualisation to create a new and more helpful neurological pathway. When I talk about visualisation in this book, it includes sounds and feelings as well as pictures and images.

There is a famous example of an Australian psychologist, Alan Richardson who worked with a team of basketball players. The players were of similar ability and the team was divided into three for the experiment. One third were told to go home and have thirty days off; one third were told to practise scoring hoops and the final third were told to visualise scoring hoops. By the end of the thirty days, they came back together. Those who had had thirty days off hadn't improved (no surprise there); those who had practised had improved and those who had visualised had also improved ... almost as much as those who had practised!

Visualisation is such a powerful tool, but why does it work? Well, it is all to do with the cognitive process that goes on when you visualise. When you visualise, you are creating a picture of a future event; this can be a still picture or a movie of you achieving your goal. As you then put sound and feelings to this image and imagine yourself achieving your goal, new neurological connections are being formed in your brain. This means that when you visualise scoring a goal or completing a presentation or becoming your ideal size, it is almost like déjà vu – as if you have already done it before in real life. Your mind already knows what it feels like, what it looks like and what it sounds like to achieve this goal. Your neurons 'light up' when you visualise, as if you are doing it right here and now.

This is why visualisation is so widely used in sport. Imagine being able to visualise scoring over and over so that when you actually play the game, you already know how – you have created what is colloquially known as muscle memory (which is actually brain memory!) You have created the new neurological pathways. The neurons fire together to create the desired response before actually completing the activity.

The great news is that you can use visualisation in many different areas of your life … it is for everyone, not just athletes.

Activity - New Behaviour Generator

One of the ways to change and create new behaviours is to use a tool called the New Behaviour Generator. This combines visualisation with the intention to create a new behaviour and gives you the ability to create a new outcome for yourself.

1. Complete your ecology check to ensure that the consequences of the change are okay in all areas of your life.

2. Close your eyes and imagine yourself as a movie director of your life. See in front of you the situation you want to change. Maybe you speak too quickly when you are nervous. Perhaps the new behaviour, you want instead, is to speak slowly and confidently or be more relaxed and charismatic when giving a presentation.

3. Play out the scenario with you performing the new behaviour while you are watching on as a movie director (we call this disassociation within NLP and is likened to when we dream or watch a home movie of ourselves). As the scene plays out, make any adjustments to ensure it is exactly how you want it to be, where you are easily and effortlessly completing the new behaviour.

4. Once you have completed watching the movie, step into the scene at the beginning and play it again, this time watching it through your own eyes. Notice how it feels; notice how other people react and check the ecology (the consequences of your new behaviour). What is the ripple effect of you behaving in that way? If, for example, your new behaviour is to present confidently, notice how you feel speaking confidently; notice how the audience reacts; notice how good it feels. This is a dress rehearsal of the situation. You are creating this new neurological pathway

so that when you actually complete the task in real life, it is as if you have that déjà vu moment – as if you have already been there before and know how to act.

5. Once you have played the movie through to the end, move back into your director chair and notice whether there is anything you need to change or anything that can be improved and check it is exactly how you want it to be. If so, you can run the movie through a number of times to really enhance your performance. If, however, you want to make changes, then do so as the movie director and repeat the process. Once you have run through the scenario as a movie director, step into the scenario and run it again, seeing it through your own eyes.

6. You can repeat this as many times as you want to until it is how you want it to be. Once you have done this, you have created new neurological pathways in terms of that new behaviour.

7. You may want to imagine some additional scenarios - for example, someone asking a question during your presentation and how you would confidently answer it. You can use this tool to practise being resilient in those situations.

This is a great technique for installing new behaviours. There is an additional technique which is also great for changing habits and compulsions – this is known as the Swish technique.

Activity – Swish

Swish is one of the famous NLP tools and works because it changes the trigger that starts the chain reaction (the very first thing you do which starts that old unwanted habit). Like that row of dominos, when you knock over the first one, the whole row will fall down.

This tool helps you to replace the trigger with something more helpful so a new neurological chain reaction occurs, rather than the old pattern of behaviour. By changing the trigger, it will result in you changing your outcome as you are creating a different neurological pathway.

1. To prepare for this technique, you need to think about the behaviour you want to change. This could be anything – switching chocolate for a healthier snack or getting out of bed rather than hitting the snooze button, for example.

2. Next you need to find the trigger. This is the very first moment when you know it is time to do your old behaviour - the start of the chain reaction.

3. Now think about the new behaviour you want instead. This new behaviour needs to meet the positive intention of the original behaviour. Remember earlier in the book when we talked about 'chunking up' to the higher-level purpose of the old behaviour. The new behaviour therefore needs to meet the higher positive intention of the original habit. You also need to think about the ecology and any secondary gains (the additional consequences of the original behaviour, which you may or may not be aware of). For example, smoking may give you extra breaks from work. Refer back to Chapter 3 for a reminder about positive intentions, ecology and secondary gains.

4. Once you have understood the trigger for the old habit, close your eyes and create a picture of that in your mind.

5. Open your eyes and think about something different or move around (we call this a break state which is a distraction that helps us to stop thinking about the old habit).

6. Create a new trigger picture of you feeling and acting differently – the new behaviour. Make sure you are seeing it through you own eyes. You can change the

submodalities of the picture to make it even better for you (see Chapter 5). Make it brighter and make it look compelling so that it is something you really want to do. Make sure the positive intention is the same as the old behaviour and that you have considered the consequences of the new behaviour and preserved any positive learnings from the old behaviour. Step out of the picture and shrink it down until it is a small dot and bursting with energy.

7. Open your eyes and move around to break your state.

8. The next part of the process is like a computer home screen with an icon on it. As you know, when you click on the icon then the home screen is totally obliterated by the new application. The same principle is used in this technique – the home screen is the old picture and the icon is the new picture which expands and completely obliterates the old picture. We complete this activity very fast and repeat it a number of times until you can no longer get the old picture back up ... this is where we are conditioning our brain to create the new neurological pathway of the new behaviour.

9. Close your eyes and bring back the old picture of the old, unwanted behaviour. Step into it so you are associated (seeing through your own eyes), and then take the new picture and place it at the bottom corner of your imaginary screen ... small and bursting with energy (just like the icon). Then say to yourself '3, 2, 1 Swish!' and as you say it, imagine that small picture exploding across the screen and totally obliterating the old picture. As you do this, move your arm from the corner (where the icon is) across the screen, at the same time as you are bringing up the new picture and say 'Swish' – a bit like a fast windscreen wiper.

10. Open your eyes so as to clear the screen and repeat again; get the old picture back up, step into the picture and then

say '3, 2, 1 Swish!' as you bring the new picture up to totally obliterate the old picture.

11. Repeat step 10 multiple times … getting faster and faster until you can no longer access the old picture and then check - how do you feel differently about the old behaviour? When you think of the original trigger, what happens now instead? When you feel differently and know that you are going to behave differently, then great… job done! If, however, you are a little uncertain, repeat the process over and over until the new pathway is really strong. As per our jungle analogy, you are creating a new pathway and the new pathway is becoming wider and clearer every time you do it.

12. Now think about a time in the future (when previously you would have done the old behaviour) and notice what happens instead.

In terms of ease of completing this activity, you may want to record yourself saying step 10 so as to guide yourself through the process. Another alternative is to find a certified NLP professional who can guide you through.

You can use this process whenever you want to make changes to behaviours and habits … to give you choice over what you say and do.

Key Learnings

The key learnings from this chapter are:

1. Visualisation enables you to create new opportunities as it gives you a 'dress rehearsal' of events and situations that are coming up – so you can have the added advantage of practising before the actual situation occurs.
2. New Behaviour Generator can be used to create new behaviours that you want.
3. Swish enables you to change the unwanted trigger of a habit (pattern of behaviours) to create a new and more helpful response and behaviour.
4. All three tools give you choice over your behaviours.

CHAPTER 8 – HOW TO CREATE EXCITING OUTCOMES

What is your purpose in life?

Why are we here? This question has been debated for centuries and I am sure will continue to be debated for centuries to come.

I think that the more useful question to ask is this: what is your personal purpose in life?

You may already know your calling in life – if so, skip this bit! If, however, you are less sure what it is, then read on! Finding your purpose is a lot simpler than you might think.

I truly believe that our purpose is to be the best version of ourselves. It's as simple as that … if you want it to be. We are all unique and have special, incredible resources which only we have. Most of us only use a small proportion of our potential and only part of the time. Applying NLP to your life can help you unleash your full potential and give you the opportunity to shine: to show the world your unique abilities, gifts and value, which the world really needs right now.

This is one of the biggest learnings in terms of NLP, in my opinion – that we are all unique. Suddenly the pressure to be right dissolves as it isn't about being 'right' or 'wrong'; it is about having a subjective view and being curious about how others see the world, as well as having the confidence to show our true, authentic selves. You can achieve your purpose in life by becoming the best version of yourself, rather than doing what you believe others think you 'should' do.

So, how do you go about becoming your true, incredible self? Well, this book will give you a great starting point to begin your amazing journey to achieve greatness in your life – whatever that means for you.

I love the phrase, 'a boat without direction is just driftwood!'

Where do you want to go in life? What does greatness mean to you?

Now, before we zoom off to start the next great thing, let's do some groundwork first and really understand what we are talking about here. There are many books which talk about setting goal after goal, being driven by ambition and moving forward no matter what. That is one approach and, I have to say, one which has served me well for a number of years. My approach now, however, is slightly different. When I talk about purpose and direction in life, I now take a gentler approach – thinking about the consequences of what I want in terms of the impact on others as well as on myself and on the planet. It is useful to know our purpose in life so we can feel fulfilled and achieve our higher-level needs and the way we go about it can be much more holistic and compassionate to ourselves, others and the world we live in.

How can we have a greater level of success?

One of the most powerful ways is to set yourself a 'well-formed outcome' so you can imagine what it is like to have already achieved your goal, giving you the benefits of having already created the neurological pathways necessary for success. The more you imagine the outcome, the better.

The first step though is to make sure you have got a great outcome or goal to begin with. If you imagine a half-eaten dinner, that is what you will get, rather than a full plate! So let me explain how we do this from an NLP perspective.

Activity - How to create a well-formed outcome

Own your goal

The outcome or goal needs to be yours – not somebody else's. It also needs to be within your reach to achieve.

I work with lots of parents who want their children to be happy. This is, of course, an awesome aspiration but it is not within their control! They can't make their children be or feel something, so they cannot influence that outcome. What would be a better outcome or goal? A more positive and useful goal might be 'to be the best parent they can be, so that their children have the right conditions to thrive and be happy'. This is something they can influence.

Ask yourself the following questions:
- Do you really want this outcome?
- Are you determined to get it?
- Can you influence the outcome?

I have worked with many people who have thought that they wanted a particular outcome and have then discovered later that it isn't their goal, but rather something they feel they 'should do' or that other people expect of them. If you want to increase your likelihood of success, make sure the outcome is something you really want.

State your goal in positive terms

Say what you want rather than what you don't want. This is really important. People often tell me what they don't want in a partner... 'I don't want them to be lazy' ... 'I don't want them to be mean' ... and guess what? When they look at their partner, they tend to find they are lazy and mean – why? Well, as we have already talked about, we get what we focus on and our RAS (Reticular Activating System) is helping us find it.

Also, we need to remember that our unconscious minds are unable to process negation, so if you say, 'I don't want to be stressed,' for example, your unconscious mind will focus on 'stressed' as we delete the 'not'. So, what you want rather than what you don't want becomes the critical element.

A question that can help you discover what you do want is, 'When you are not stressed, what are you?' The answer might be calm, relaxed or happy. Therefore, when you are thinking about your outcome, make sure it is written in a way that states what you do want rather than what you don't want.

Your goal is starting to become well-formed; you have made sure it is owned by you; it states what you want (rather than what you don't want); and you have checked it is something that you really do want, rather than something someone else is expecting you to do.

Consider the consequences of the outcome

The next step is to check on the ecology around your outcome by considering the consequences of achieving your goals. What will you gain or lose by achieving your outcome?

Building on what you have already learnt, ask yourself the following great questions (called the Cartesian Co-ordinates):

1. What will happen when you achieve your outcome?
2. What won't happen when you achieve your outcome?
3. What will happen if you don't achieve your outcome?
4. What won't happen if you don't achieve your outcome?

When you answer each of these questions, you will have a greater understanding of the ecology of your outcome and be able to manage the consequences more easily. It also helps to flush out any unintended consequences you may not be aware of and anything that could derail your goal.

Let's work through an example. Say your goal is to become healthier and be a size 12 by Christmas.

1. *What will happen when you achieve your goal?*
   You will have lost weight.
   Your health issues will have reduced.
   You will have become healthier.
   You will be able to wear the clothes you want.

2. *What won't happen when you achieve your goal?*
    You won't have health issues.
    You won't be miserable about your size.
    You won't comfort eat in the evenings.

3. *What will happen if you don't achieve it?*
    You will have potential health problems.
    You will feel bad about your weight.
    You will have to buy new clothes for Christmas.

4. *What won't happen if you don't achieve it?*
    You won't have to exercise or go on a diet.
    You won't have to give up the foods you like.

By looking at the answers, you can start to see them as balances on scales. Do the positive consequences of achieving your goal outweigh the negative consequences of not achieving it? If eating what you like and shopping for new clothes outweighs exercising and eating healthily, the chances of success will be reduced significantly. It is then that we can put contingency plans in place to make the goal more appealing. For example, you can still go shopping for new clothes that fit your new figure or you can find an exercise you really love rather than following the crowd and doing something you hate. By identifying and addressing the consequences of your actions before you start, your chances of success will be greatly increased.

As we think about the consequences, we also need to consider any secondary gains. For example, does being unhealthy give you useful excuses ... to not go out when you don't want to ... to have additional time off work if you are sick ... to have lots of sympathy from others? These can be powerful drivers to keep you where you are, rather than help you move forward. What other ways can the needs of the secondary gain be met in a more positive way? For example, how much more empowering would it be to gain attention by helping others rather than gaining attention by having people feel sorry for you? How much easier would it be to be honest if you don't want to go out, rather than make up health-related excuses? You get the picture, I'm sure.

When you understand the positive intention of any habit you wish to change, you can ensure that your new activities will give you the same positive outcome as the old, unwanted habit. Ensuring that the positive intention of the new activity and the positive intention of the old habit are aligned, will give you a greater chance of success.

Use your senses to help you imagine your goal

As discussed in Chapter 7, to be able to visualise your outcome effectively, you need to know how it will look, sound and feel when you have achieved your goal.

In your mind, go to the date when you will have achieved your outcome. Notice what you see – maybe the new weight on your scales. Notice what you hear – perhaps people are paying you compliments or maybe you are congratulating yourself. Notice what you feel – what are the emotions that are there when you have achieved your goal? As discussed in Chapter 7, visualisation is almost like déjà vu – it is as if you have already done it before in real life and will therefore increase your chance of success.

Finally, remember to take action. Action turns your dreams and aspirations into reality. What is your first step? When are you going to take it?

Goals and outcomes are great and remember to also think about the experiences you want too. Enjoy the process of achieving your outcomes and remember to celebrate your success. In my world, a holiday starts with the flight rather than when you arrive at your destination. So enjoy the flight ... otherwise you may be too busy and miss living your life!

Key Learnings

The key learnings from this chapter are:

1. Understand your purpose in life ... to be the best version of you!
2. Create time to visualise how you want your life to be – from small changes through to bigger outcomes.
3. Make sure all your outcomes are well-formed:
    a. Say what you want rather than what you don't want.
    b. Make sure the goals and outcomes are owned by you and within your control to achieve.
    c. Understand the positive intention behind your old behaviour and ensure it is aligned in terms of your new outcome.
    d. Make sure the outcome is yours and not someone else's goal.
    e. Make sure you really do want it and you are determined to achieve it.
    f. Ensure you have considered the consequences of your outcome, taking into consideration any secondary gains and unintended consequences and make plans to overcome these.
    g. Remember to take action.
4. Remember to think about the experiences you want in life rather than always focusing on the next outcome.
5. Remember to enjoy the flight!

PART TWO - ENJOYING THE FLIGHT OF YOUR LIFE!

Part One of this book is all about changing unwanted beliefs, behaviours and emotions to give us more control and choice within our lives so that we can become the best version of ourselves.

Part Two is all about making NLP a part of your everyday life on an ongoing basis, so you can continue to grow and create the life you desire. It is likely that after making some initial changes in Part One, you will notice even more choices that are available to you as you move forward. Now you have started your journey of self-discovery, more things are likely to appear that you may want to change ... it really is an ongoing process, so feel free to dip back into Part One now and then.

In this next part of the book, you will learn:
- how to look after yourself
- how to create the incredible life you desire
- how to discover your true potential and your own unique abilities.

During the next chapters, we will be focusing on a model of SELF-CARE – a tool kit for how to use NLP to improve your quality of life and to equip you for whatever life throws at you.

Using SELF-CARE as an acronym, we will take each of the letters in turn:
- **S**pace
- **E**nergy
- **L**anguage
- **F**lexibility
- **C**larity
- **A**ttitude
- **R**elationships
- **E**xciting Future

As George Eliot said, 'It is never too late to be what you might have been.' This is certainly great news for us all!

What is self-care?

It is a term that is used more and more and is becoming critically important to create balance in our busy world. I have heard some people refer to it as selfish ... I guess that is one perspective. The way I look at it is similar to when we are in an aeroplane and are told that we need to put on our oxygen mask first, before helping others. If we don't look after ourselves, then how are we going to be resourceful enough to look after those we care about? Taking the time to look after ourselves, even if it is only a couple of minutes a day, is so important.

As with many things in life, it can be useful to look at it as a continuum: at one end are those who are great at self-care and at the other are those who neglect themselves. I am sure, like me, you find yourself moving along that continuum and being in different places at different times.

Self-care is about being kind to ourselves, listening to our bodies and our unconscious mind and then moving forward. So, let's learn how ...

CHAPTER 9 - CREATING SPACE IN YOUR LIFE

The first element of our SELF-CARE model is space. What do I mean by space? I mean the physical space within which we live. I also mean mental space – giving yourself some time to reflect and meditate so that you can look at your life in a more holistic way and consciously decide your direction.

Physical space

In terms of physical space, it is important that we separate our work life from our home life. As you know from the chapter on emotions, we have triggers that generate emotions through what we see, hear, smell, taste and feel. So, when you see your laptop, you are likely to think about work. Making a clear separation, therefore, can really help you to relax. Even if you are working at a kitchen table during the day, make sure you pack away your work things in the evening (as these are your 'work anchors'), so that you are not constantly reminded of work whilst you are relaxing.

Time to breathe

Life can move at such a fast pace that we can forget to slow down and take some time to think about where we want to go, rather than just rushing headlong into the next thing. I know many people who go from goal to goal – I used to be one of them. Goals are amazing, as long as they take you closer to your purpose in life – to be the best version of you! Sometimes, however, when we are so focused on our goals, we can actually miss the life that is going on all around us ... this has taken me a long time to realise! I still have exciting goals, but I take more time now to enjoy the ride and to celebrate when I've reached them. How many times have you achieved a goal and then moved straight onto the next one without really appreciating your achievement?

One of the ways I remind myself to do this is by setting well-formed outcomes (see Chapter 8) and then identifying exactly what activities I need to do to achieve that outcome. Once I have established this, I focus every day on the activities I have planned and fully enjoy and embrace these, rather than keep looking at the goal, so that I can enjoy the process and celebrate the outcome.

An important part of the 'space' element is to take the time to appreciate what you already have. There are a number of ways to do this. Meditation and mindfulness are great tools to enable us to appreciate what is happening around us, slow down and be present. Another powerful technique is the Core Transformation Process, by Connirae Andreas which is a beautiful, gentle and powerful process to enable us to come to wholeness and spiritual awakening. These tools help to build your internal sense of self – to build a strong core – so that whatever happens in life, you have a firm base to move forward from. When you discover your true identity, you can be comfortable in your own skin and create the space to be who you truly are.

See www.achieveyourgreatness.co.uk for information on Identity By Design, NLP and Core Transformation courses.

Regularly giving yourself space is so important. Even a couple of minutes a day (just before you get up in the morning to think about all the things you are grateful for), can really set the tone of your day.

We only truly have this moment in time – everything in the future we don't yet know about. We can guess or 'make up' what is going to happen, but it is just 'made up'. None of us know for certain what is around the corner. Therefore, as I've said before, if we are going to predict the future, let's predict something good! If we are going to make stuff up, let's make it 'good stuff' and also let's take the time to visualise what that 'good stuff' will look like.

Learning

Learning is such a key element in terms of self-care. Have you ever wondered what made Einstein so incredibly intelligent? Did he have a bigger brain than the rest of us? Did he have more neurological connections? What was his secret? Well, one thing we do know is that he was pretty clever and most of us would like to have some of that too!

One of the ways we can ensure that we can be as clever as we want to be is to give ourselves the space to continuously learn – to stretch ourselves and to create those new neurological connections. But what has that got to do with self-care and why should we bother?

Well, it is widely accepted that education is the basis for getting a good job, earning more money and having a better lifestyle. It doesn't end there though. Let's consider the wider benefits of learning in terms of what it does for us from a neurological perspective.

We looked at visualisation in Part One of the book, where we learnt about the power of our mind in terms of muscle (mind) memory. There has been recent research about the benefits of learning … which are far more than just helping us to become clever!

Recent research found that learning to dance is great at slowing down the advances of dementia and can keep us young. Why? Because dancing uses the logical, mathematical and scientific elements of our brain as well as the creative and the artistic part. When we learn to dance, we are improving our fitness, health, balance and posture as well as coordination. It also improves our ability to learn faster. In terms of the mind and body connection, we are changing our physiology when we dance. As you know, one of the ways to change how you feel quickly and easily is to change your physiology. So, if you are learning to dance, it is helping you in terms of mental ability as well as from an emotional and physical perspective – pretty cool!

Have you noticed that if you are feeling low and then go out for a walk, your mood is much better? Well, (as we discovered in

Chapter 2 on the NLP Communication Model,) this is because our physiology is connected to how we feel. So, if we learn a new physical activity, this has multiple benefits.

That is not to say other forms of learning don't have equally important benefits. If you learn a new instrument, for example, this will help with memory and hand to eye coordination. Learning a language can also help develop strong cognitive skills such as mental flexibility, listening, problem solving and social interaction.

Learning has such great benefits from a physical and mental perspective because new neurological connections are created. As we learn new things, we open our minds to new horizons, learning new skills, discovering new possibilities and ultimately stretching our 'map of the world'. Of all the things I personally have learnt, NLP has given me the greatest benefit in terms of well-being and how to live a better life.

Learning something new can sometimes be a less than easy process when you first start. Remember, there is no such thing as failure, only feedback. What can you learn from the process of learning that you can take forward and use in your future? As discussed in Part One, when things don't go as planned, this can be when innovation and new ideas can take shape.

Learning is stretching your 'map of the world' – expanding your experience to enable you to have a richer life and experience. To learn something new keeps you mentally alert and gives you an opportunity to discover new and exciting things. In terms of self-care this is critical as it helps give you purpose. There is always balance – remembering to rest and relax as well.

Sometimes learning and relaxation can be combined. When I learnt to play the saxophone, I had to concentrate so hard I switched off totally from everything else – a great time to immerse myself in learning and be completely present in the moment. If you learn crafting or painting, for example, this can have a double benefit too.

Key Learnings

The key learnings from this chapter are:

1. Give yourself space from a physical as well as mental perspective.
2. Ensure that your physical space supports you – have different zones or spaces for different activities.
3. Meditation and mindfulness is a great way to give yourself some mental space to enable you to be more present.
4. Use visualisation to create the future you want.
5. Continuous learning keeps us mentally (and physically) healthy.

CHAPTER 10 – MANAGING YOUR ENERGY

The first 'E' in my SELF-CARE framework is energy, which is fundamental to our existence. In this context, I am referring to balance in terms of how we manage our energy.

When we think about energy, we have 3 main elements:
- What we do to generate energy (the food and drink that we consume)
- How we expend energy (through exercise, work and activities)
- How we recover and restore our energy (through sleep, rest and relaxation).

It is all about balance – if one of these areas is out of balance, this will impact on our physical and mental well-being.

If we consume too much energy (or the wrong kind) and don't do enough to burn it off, we will put on weight. If we are expending too much energy and not resting, then our bodies haven't had enough time to recover and restore. Each element is equally important and needs our attention.

A very good friend of mine (an Occupational Therapist) has a great analogy in terms of energy: she suggests we need to manage our energy like a budget – how much are we putting into our account, how much are we taking out and how are we spending our energy? Getting the balance right is key to our well-being.

This is not rocket science but for many it is an area that can be less than easy to balance. I know from my own experience that I can focus on one area and maybe neglect another (by working really hard on a project and not having enough sleep, for example). We can manage like this for a while but if we continue like this for too long, it can be detrimental to both our physical and mental well-being.

How can we manage our energy better?

a. Create a routine

A good tip is to create a routine for yourself. When it comes to self-care and well-being, I have found that when I don't have a routine, then it doesn't happen. A great book *Miracle Morning* by Hal Elrod gives you a sequence of things to do in the morning to set yourself up for success.

When we are going through times of uncertainty, routine becomes even more important. It doesn't need to be long or extensive and there can always be flexibility. When you have choice within that routine, you are more likely to stick with it.

Apparently, in the US Army, the first thing they do every day is make their bed. Why? Because before their day has even started, they have already completed something. Having quick wins is really important, especially in times of stress as these are the little things we can control. When lots of things happen, which we feel are outside our control, this can generate a feeling of overwhelm and stress, which can lead to a stress response – the fight, flight or freeze reaction. When this response is triggered, the amygdala is working overtime and the connection to the frontal cortex (the logical thinking part of the brain) doesn't work so well. As we have already discovered, this can have a detrimental impact on our mental and physical well-being. It is important, therefore, to learn how to manage our response so that we can have a better outcome ... quick wins is just one way.

Although routine is helpful, it is less helpful to beat ourselves up when things don't go to plan. We have busy lives and we are all human. It's ok if you don't always stick to the routine so cut yourself some slack. Ask what you want to learn from the day and then look forward and set your sights on what you want the next day to look like instead.

I like to adopt the Pareto principle – the 80/20 rule. 80% of the time you follow the routine and 20% of the time you let yourself off the hook! It is all about choices and priorities ... maybe it is about time some of the elements you have ignored up to now are considered. If we are not listening to our bodies, our unconscious mind can bring about something to make us listen. Have you ever had the situation where you have worked for a long stretch and then went on holiday and were unwell? If so, that is your unconscious mind's way of getting you to stop and relax. How much better would it be to listen to your body before you became unwell?

b. Take a holiday in your mind

One of my good friends talks about going on a holiday in her mind for 1 minute per hour. Once an hour may be a bit much for some of us but taking a little bit of time out once a day to visualise and remember the times when you were on holiday is a great start. Taking yourself back to that time and seeing what you saw, hearing what you heard and feeling what you felt (or even just looking at a photo of a great time) can give you a real boost. Listening to a favourite song is also an awesome way to change how you feel.

As you know, in NLP we call this an anchor (see Chapter 6 for a reminder). You can use visual anchors (such as a photo), auditory anchors (such as a favourite song) and kinaesthetic anchors (such as a hug). These automatic responses can naturally change your state by firing off positive neurological connections, helping you to relax and feel better.

c. Eat well

How many times have we heard of people, who have started a new diet, gone off the rails for one meal and then never gone back on the plan? Instead, it would be better to let go of the day that didn't go to plan and then reset your focus for the next day, rather than feeling guilty and giving up.

Our bodies are beautiful machines. Think of your body like a car – if you put petrol in a diesel car, things don't go so well. We need to provide enough nutrition for us to maintain a healthy lifestyle. Knowing your own body and listening to what it needs is so important. For example, do you really know when you are hungry? Or are you actually thirsty? The sensations can easily be confused. Making time to ensure that we prepare and eat healthy meals is important.

d. Get moving

My advice is this: find something you love and do that! Many people have a gym membership and never actually go to the gym. Unfortunately, that won't get anyone fitter! What do you love doing? Maybe it is swimming, walking, yoga, squash or cycling - whatever it is, spend your time doing that. If you are not keen on exercise, then combine it with something you do love. For example, I don't find being on a cross-trainer exciting but combine it with reading a good book or watching a movie and time flies!

Our mind and body are connected – we are one cybernetic loop (one system). For many years, it was thought that what happens in our mind is completely separate to what is physically happening to us. This has more recently been disproved via psychoneuroimmunology and other research.

e. Rest

One way we expend our energy is through work – whether that is sorting out the house or running your business or working for an employer. Again, balance is key. Taking regular breaks is a great idea as is breaking your work up into manageable chunks. Writing a to-do list to check off items as you go can really help with motivation.

A famous metaphor that is useful to remember is the one of the master woodcutter and his apprentice. The apprentice was nearing the end of his apprenticeship with the master woodcutter and on this day, the master woodcutter said they would see how much wood the apprentice could chop. So, both the master and apprentice started chopping wood – they carried on all day. The apprentice was working really hard, chopping and chopping. Every now and then he would look over to the master and noticed he was sitting there resting. The apprentice worked harder and harder until finally the last piece of wood had been cut. He went over to the master woodcutter and they compared the piles of wood. The apprentice had cut a big pile of wood, which he was really pleased about. He then went to see the Master Woodcutter's pile … which was huge and much bigger than his.

'I don't understand,' said the apprentice. 'I saw you sitting, taking it easy, having breaks, drinking tea … you weren't working nearly as hard as me. How come your pile is so much bigger?'

'Well,' said the Master Woodcutter. 'I remembered to sharpen my axe.'

So, what are you doing to sharpen your axe? Applying the tools in this book is a great start.

We need to be in touch with our bodies to know when we need to rest – when to take it easy, put our feet up or just do something we love.

So, what do you love to do – chat to your friends, share a meal with others, walk in nature, play with your pets, do your favourite hobby, help others, give back? Doing what you love helps you to achieve balance and have a rounder and more fulfilled life.

f.   Look after your immune system

We have already looked at nutrition, exercise and rest – one of the other key things to learn is how to manage our thoughts and the stress response.

As we are a cybernetic loop, what we think impacts on our physiology and can impact on our immune system, so it is a jolly good idea to look after both our physical and mental health.

People seem to be drawn to one or the other, but we need to look after both – we need to exercise, put the right foods into our bodies and also look after our mental well-being. This is where NLP comes in. As you already know from Part One, NLP gives us the tools to enable us to manage our emotions, behaviours and habits more easily.

g. Sleep

There is a lot of research about the importance of sleep and how much we need to keep healthy. A great book on the subject is *Why We Sleep* by Matthew Walker – a fascinating read and highly recommended. The impact of sleep on our mental and physical health is enormous and NLP can really help. Ensure you give yourself the adequate opportunity to sleep.

Visit www.achieveyourgreatness.co.uk for more information and support on this topic.

h. Taking on someone else's energy

Have you ever noticed how sometimes you can enter a room and feel the energy – whether that is positive or negative? We are all energetic beings. In other words, we transmit energy to others all the time. Remember the last time you met someone who was in a bad mood and how that felt.

Some people find that they take on board other people's energy and carry it with them. Well, this next activity enables you to clear any energy that isn't yours. This allows you to enjoy your own energy in a clean and pure way.

To be clear, you can still be empathetic but if you take on someone else's energy, this is disempowering for them and you. To really help someone, you need to be feeling resourceful (remember the difference between empathy and sympathy that I mentioned before).

Activity – clearing energy from others

1. Take a moment to sit or stand quietly and close your eyes.

2. Notice any energy that you are holding that belongs to someone else and notice where you hold that energy in or around you.

3. Imagine sending that energy to the centre of the earth for recycling.

4. Repeat 2 and 3 for all the energy you are feeling that isn't yours.

5. Once you have let go of all the energy that isn't yours, take a moment to reconnect with your own energy. Allow that to build up inside of you – that good, pure, clean energy – and allow it to flow throughout your body.

6. Open your eyes and notice how that feels.

If you want to discover more about Energetic NLP, Art Giser is the creator and an expert in this field.

Key Learnings

The key learnings from this chapter are:

1. Think of your energy like a budget ... how do you want to spend it?
2. Learn how to manage your thoughts and stress levels as it impacts on well-being and the immune system (psychoneuroimmunology).
3. Ensure a balance of energy by:
   - Creating a routine and focusing on quick wins to support well-being
   - Eating healthily
   - Exercising regularly
   - Managing workload
   - Making sure you take the time (and space) to rest, sleep and relax.
4. Anchoring enables you to change your state and feel better whenever you want to (see Chapter 6).
5. Notice if you are taking on someone else's energy and remember to clear it on a regular basis.

CHAPTER 11 – MINDING YOUR LANGUAGE

In this chapter we are going to be talking about the importance of our language. Many people go through life using language without really thinking about what they are saying and the power of their words. Words are not just words ... they are so much more than that. They fire off neurological connections in your brain and can support or damage situations and relationships.

Our language is a reflection of our thoughts. Therefore, when you really listen carefully to what another person is saying, you can get a more accurate picture of what is happening for that person at that point in time.

I'm sure you have heard the phrase 'active listening' where you are really paying attention to what another person is saying. This is different from listening at a surface level where you are thinking about what you want to say next, rather than being wholly engaged with what the other person is saying - listening, without judgement but with curiosity and understanding. This is key to successful relationships, communication and negotiations within all areas of your life.

We have already seen the power of language when we looked at the Mercedes Model earlier on in the book and talked about the 'strong like superman' activity. We know the power of our language impacts on our physiology and the language we use is a reflection of our focus (i.e. our thoughts). This mind-body connection is so powerful that it impacts on our immune system (psychoneuroimmunology). Language isn't just words.

When we consciously change what we are saying, we can choose words that directly impact what our RAS finds for us, which will positively affect our outcomes. We can avoid our RAS finding all the things we don't want and we can start to use positive language to get those things we do want and start to create the life we desire.

How can we change our language to get more positive outcomes?

a. Say what you can do, not what you can't do

This is especially important in business. You will be surprised how many companies fall into this trap – they get an enquiry and rather than saying, 'yes we can do this for you in January', they say 'sorry, we can't do it before Christmas.' The first one feels so much more positive and gives the client confidence in the company's ability.

Normally, this happens because we are so caught up in our map of the world that we are not listening effectively to what is actually being asked of us, so we jump to conclusions. Next time somebody asks something of you, take a moment to really listen to what the person needs. Step out of your map and into their map. Say what you can do to help rather than what you can't do. Early in his career, Richard Branson learnt to always say 'yes' and then found out how to do it afterwards. It is much more empowering to have a 'yes' from a company than a 'no'. If you really can't do it, then find a way of still helping them; refer on, for example. I talk more about the word 'can't' later in this chapter.

b. Say what you want, not what you don't want

I'm sure we have all seen signs that say: DON'T WALK ON THE GRASS. As you know, our unconscious minds cannot process negation and so will only process 'walk on the grass.' It is clearer and more empowering to say: PLEASE WALK ON THE PATH.

So, start to say what you want rather than what you don't want. It will help your RAS start to find what you are looking for.

c. Avoid the word 'if'

The word 'if' can create doubt and can have three meanings – 'if and I will', 'if and I won't' and 'if and maybe I will and maybe I won't'. In English, we only have the one word for 'if' and we have to guess the meaning. Normally we mean 'if and maybe I will and maybe I won't'. For example, 'I'll make you a coffee if I have time,' would probably leave you with a bit of doubt as to whether I will make you a coffee or not! It would be better, therefore, to say, 'When I have time, I will make you a coffee'. It is even better to provide a timescale though – saying you will get something done by a certain date and then delivering early. So, a better phrase would be 'I'll make you a coffee at 3pm' and have it delivered just before.

You may, however, choose to use 'if' intentionally, when you want to create doubt or there is uncertainty around a situation. For example, 'if tomorrow it is sunny, we will go to the beach'.

d. Avoid the word 'but'

The word 'but' is another word which is good to eliminate or upgrade. When we hear the word 'but,' everything before it is negated. An example could be, 'It was a great presentation, but it was too long'. The part you are likely to remember is that 'it was too long'.

You can do one of two things:
- Use 'but' with intention. For example, 'It was long, but it was a great presentation'.
- Use 'and' instead or a full stop. For example, 'It was a great presentation, and it was a long presentation'.

Using 'but' can be a good habit to break. I have heard so many people say 'I love him but ...'

So, is it time for a language upgrade? Whether via email, messages or everyday chat – remove the 'buts' and see how it changes things!

e.   Avoid the word 'try'

The other word to upgrade is 'try'. Like the word 'if', it creates doubt.

'I'll try and do it for you' doesn't leave you with much confidence that I will do whatever it is you want.

The issue is that when we use 'try,' not only does the other person lose confidence, the word also creates uncertainty for ourselves. We need to be clear and direct when we communicate with our unconscious mind about what we want. Saying 'I will try' to do something is full of doubt but saying 'I will do something' not only instils confidence in the other person, it also sends a clear message to your unconscious mind that you mean business and you are determined to succeed. So, change 'I will try' to 'I will'.

f.   Listen out for the word 'can't' in yourself and in others

Just by listening to what people say gives you a great insight into what is going on for them: what internal beliefs they hold about themselves, the world and how things should or shouldn't be. For example, phrases like 'I can't' let us know that they have a limiting belief about themselves.

Have a listen to your own language and note the times you find yourself saying you can't do something – then refer to the beliefs chapter and look to change any beliefs that aren't serving you.

Upgrade to, 'I can't do that *yet*' or 'I haven't learnt how to do that *yet*', or even better, 'Once I practise more, I will be able to do that'. This will all serve to support a healthy belief system.

g.   Listen out for 'shoulds'

If you find yourself saying 'I shouldn't...' or 'I've got to...' ask, 'what would happen if you did?' or 'what would happen if you didn't?' respectively. Again, these tiny words can indicate strong beliefs which might be holding you back from doing what you want or indicate that you are living by someone else's rules.

h.   Avoid 'why?'

'Why did you do that?' is often met with defensiveness. The other person feels that they are backed into a corner and therefore feel that they have to defend themselves.

'So, what just happened?' is far more likely to create a better outcome as the other person will feel that you are prepared to listen to their side of the story.

How can you speak to someone so it resonates with them more easily?

a.   Match their preferred way to process information

If you remember back to the NLP Communication Model, we talked about how we take our information in via our five senses – visual, auditory, kinaesthetic, olfactory and gustatory. In the same way, we have preferences in terms of how we process information, as well as how we communicate information to other people. We are given clues to other people's preferences through the words they use.

Somebody with a visual preference might say. 'I *see* what you mean' or '*show* me your ideas'.

A person with an auditory preference, might use words such as 'I *hear* what you are *saying*,' 'let's *sound* out that idea' or 'that *resonates* with me'.

If they have a kinaesthetic (feelings) preference, they will use words such as '*walk* me through how this works' or 'it doesn't *feel* right'.

Olfactory predicates are words such as 'that *smells* fishy' and gustatory words are those such as 'that leaves a bad *taste* in my mouth'.

You may also find people who have an auditory digital preference which is a more analytical, self-talk preference. They would use words such as 'does that *make sense* to you?' or 'do you *understand*?'

These words are called predicates and they are words that give us clues as to a person's preference.

If you are working with a group of people, for example, and you are not sure on their preference, present your information so it meets a range of preferences. You might use pictures and diagrams, as well as a voice-over and activities for them to do to apply the knowledge. If this isn't possible for whatever reason, stick to auditory digital predicates as most people can relate to these more easily.

The art of great communication is reducing resistance and we do that by building rapport. When we are flexible in terms of our approach and provide the other person with the information in a way that suits them, it is like going to France and speaking French rather than shouting in English and expecting people to understand! So ideally, know what their preference is and use the words that resonate with them.

b. Reflect their words back to them

Reflecting back using their exact words is also a really effective way to communicate with others as it fires off their specific neurological pathways (rather than trying to change them to meet your map of the world). For example, if someone says that something is 'gripping' use their word 'gripping,' rather than interpreting it as 'exciting' as it may not mean the same thing for them. This helps to lower resistance and shows you are really listening to what they are saying.

c. Check whether you are mindreading

Are you attaching meaning to what they have said based on your map of the world?

For example, imagine someone tells you that they are 'really busy'. It can be tempting to jump in with an answer such as:

'Awesome, that's great news' (one perspective)

Or

'Really? I'm so sorry' (another perspective).

These are both mind-reads and projections of our own

perspective. Instead, we can be curious and find out their meaning. Is being busy a good or bad thing for them or is it just a statement? We can find out by asking great open clean questions such as, 'How is that for you?' to discover their perspective.

Let's look at another example. Imagine somebody says, 'I'm really tired. I didn't sleep last night.'

Instead of saying, 'Wow, that's awful. You poor thing,' ask the open question, 'Really? What happened?'

Maybe they were travelling on holiday.

Maybe they were partying all night ... we don't know as we weren't there!

So, instead of mindreading and assuming we know what they mean, we need to really listen to what a person is saying and be curious, rather than jumping to conclusions.

I had a boss once who used to have a saying: 'If you 'assume', you make an Ass out of U and Me!'

Instead, go round to their side first. Really listen to what they are saying, ask open or clean questions to lower resistance and build rapport (see Chapter 15 on rapport).

Note: David Grove created Clean Language which is a set of questions that prevents us from projecting our map of the world onto others, by keeping our questions 'clean'. For example: what just happened? What do you want to happen? How do you know?

Key Learnings

The key learnings from this chapter are:

1. 'If', 'but', 'try' – upgrade these to 'when', 'and', 'will'.
2. Avoid asking 'why' and ask open clean questions instead.
3. Remember, the unconscious mind can't process negation so say what you want rather than what you don't want.
4. Remember what you are saying is a reflection of what you are thinking, so upgrading your language has an impact on your neurological connections and physiology.
5. Listen out for predicates and the person's preference – use this language to build rapport and lower resistance.
6. Ensure you are not mindreading – ask good, clean questions to ensure you really understand their meaning, rather than assuming.

CHAPTER 12 – FLEXIBILITY AND CREATIVITY: KEYS TO RESILIENCE

Flexibility goes hand in hand with creativity and is important because it is one of the keys to resilience. We need to be flexible in our thinking in order for us to be creative. If we are rigid in our thinking, we will be less likely to have new ideas or new ways of working or looking at things. Let me give you an example. Remember when we were talking about the distortion filter in the NLP Communication Model. Well, we said that this is also known as the creativity filter because it is about taking a different angle or perspective on something – illustrated by the post-it note company I mentioned before. If they hadn't been flexible, they would have binned the glue for 'not working' rather than looking at it in a more flexible and creative way to come up with a new product that has had many years of success.

The more flexible and creative we are, the more resilient we will be when life throws us a curve ball. Let's take the Covid pandemic as an example. Many found themselves suddenly having to home-school the children whilst simultaneously doing their usual 9-5 jobs from home. Those who were flexible and went with it – coming up with innovative ideas of how to balance these various activities – found the experience of lockdown less of an ordeal than those who were trying to work in the same way as before, while juggling the additional challenges.

A friend of mine had two small children and lived in a flat in London during the lockdown. Due to family illness, his 2 and 4-year-old children didn't leave the flat the entire time. However, every weekend they went on a new adventure – from tobogganing, skiing, camping – you name it ... all indoors! Admittedly, he is a scout leader, however, this was incredible! He also worked from home, running his busy companies. Whenever we chatted, he had a new adventure and positive outcomes to share. That really is creativity and flexibility at its best – creating beautiful and wonderful memories for the family, even during such a challenging time.

Creativity seems to have been a hot topic for a number of years now with employers wanting this as a 'key skill'. So, what does it mean? Well, when we look at creativity, we are considering it from the following perspectives:

1. Doing and making things (the more traditional view of creativity)
2. Coming up with new ideas (innovation).

They both require flexibility. You may have the most amazing idea and if it doesn't quite go to plan the first time, your idea won't get off the ground unless you are flexible.

Remember the NLP presupposition: the element in the system with the most flexibility is the catalyst of the system. With the example I gave of my friend, he was the catalyst in the system. The event was the same for him as for everybody else – it was outside his control. However, he chose to focus on what he could do to make lockdown fun for his children. He had a great time too, by the way!

So, flexibility and creativity are essential for resilience so that you can bounce back from unexpected events by coming up with solutions to enable you to ensure your mental and physical well-being are looked after during tough times. This is key to self-care.

One thing that many people find less easy is dealing with uncertainty – the not knowing what is going to happen. Well, when we are creative and flexible then we can take back control of things within our remit and therefore move forward more easily. You could draw around your hand and write all the things that are within you control on the inside and all the things that are outside your control on the outside. This is a great way to start to help you to refocus on what is within your control and will help to reduce the feeling of overwhelm.

How can we become more creative?

Well practice is one way. As you know, when we practise a skill, we create new neurological pathways in our minds – the more we practise, the stronger the pathways become. Remember the first time you rode a bike or drove a car. You probably had to focus consciously on everything you were doing – looking, signalling and manoeuvring. After a while, you become more used to these things and you start to do them unconsciously. Have you ever driven somewhere and then wondered how you got there? Well, that is your unconscious mind at work. You now have what is referred to as unconscious competence.

The path to unconscious competence looks like this:
1. Conscious incompetence (the first few times you drive)
2. Conscious competence (ready to take your test and pass)
3. Unconscious competence (you can drive well without thinking about it).

There is a fourth element called unconscious incompetence. These are the things you do automatically and are not very good at (without consciously being aware). This is why, especially in business, it is useful to get feedback from a wide variety of clients and colleagues so that you can evaluate the new information and think about what you want to do about it – is there an area you can improve on?

Activity – Disney Creativity Strategy

I consider Walt Disney to be one of the most creative people in history. Robert Dilts, one of the greats in the NLP world, modelled Walt Disney's creativity strategy, which I want to share with you. By learning from other creatives, we too can become even more creative.

There are three distinct elements to the strategy:
1. The Dreamer State
2. The Realist State
3. The Critic State.

Each of these elements need to be considered separately (and in this order) to gain the true benefit from the strategy and for a creative solution to be discovered.

This strategy combines a number of techniques, including anchoring.

We will create spatial anchors, so you will need a little bit of room. Get three pieces of paper and write the above states on them: 'Dreamer', 'Realist', 'Critic' (one on each piece of paper). Lay these three pieces of paper on the floor in the shape of a triangle.

1. Stand just in front of the piece of paper with 'Dreamer' written on. We are going to anchor this state. Think of a time when you felt really creative – a time when ideas just flowed and you really loved being creative. If this is less than easy for you, then you can just imagine (act 'as if') what it would be like to feel that way. See what you see, hear what you hear, say what you say to yourself when you are feeling really creative. When you reach an 8 on the scale of 1 to 10 (where 10 is super creative), step forward onto the piece of paper and continue to increase that feeling of creativity until you reach a 10. Then step off the paper marker. You can then test the anchor to make sure it is strong by stepping on to the marker and seeing how it feels ... are you feeling creative? If so, great. If not, then repeat until you have created a strong 'dreamer' anchor. (See Chapter 6 if you need a refresher on anchoring).

2. The next element is called the 'Realist' state – so this is the planning and organising space. In the same way as you did with the creative anchor, create a 'realist' anchor on the next piece of paper. Think of a time when you felt super organised. See what you see when you are really organised, hear what you hear when you are really organised, and say what you say to yourself when you are really organised. Grow this feeling until it is stronger and stronger and throughout all your body, and then step forward onto the 'realist' paper marker on the floor and

allow that feeling to grow even more. Then take a step off the paper for a moment and step back and test that it is strong enough. If you need it stronger, then repeat again.

3. The third element is called the 'Critic' and this is where you critically evaluate the ideas and make a judgement in terms of what will work, what would need to change, the risks and opportunities as well as what you could do to mitigate or take advantage of these (like a critical friend). Create an anchor for this one in the same way as before with a time when you felt that you were really good at challenging constructively. Build those feelings as before and when they are really strong, step onto the marker on the floor. Make those feelings even stronger and then, once they are really strong, step off the marker for a moment and go back and test by stepping back into the 'critic' space and notice how that feels ... again, repeat if necessary until it is a really strong anchor for you.

4. Now you have created each of these anchors on the ground, the next step is to consider the area where you want to become more creative. Think about the outcome you want and then step into the 'Dreamer' space and start to come up with ideas around your issue or problem. Remember to focus only on coming up with ideas ... it doesn't matter how wild or wacky they are. Keep on coming up with new ideas ... even when you think you have run out of ideas, give yourself time and go further to create more exciting suggestions. Remember the realist and critic stages come later. At this stage it is all about coming up with ideas rather than thinking about how they are going to be implemented or whether they are practical.

5. Once you have come up with some great ideas, take the best suggestion forward into the next position which is that of the 'Realist'. Step into this space and start to think about what needs to happen; the plans that need to be put into place for the idea to be a success and the

sequence and logical steps needed. This enables you to put a rough outline of a plan in place.

6. Then, and only once you have completed the previous stage, step into the 'Critic' space and challenge the ideas and plans in a constructive way. What would work/ wouldn't work? What is missing? What is unnecessary? What would need to change to make it work? This then ensures your ideas are robust.

    The order you do this is really important. If you have the 'Critic' before the 'Realist' then the judgements are being made before the full details have been thought through. Without the 'Dreamer' element, there will be no new ideas to work on. Without the realist, the ideas remain just ideas - dreams with no substance or plans to enable them to become a reality.

7. Once you have gone around the three elements in turn, then you can go back into the 'Dreamer' space. Take the finalised plan back into this creative space to add some more creative ideas to the plan, especially if required to overcome any of the risks identified in the 'Critic' space and how to change the idea to ensure it will work.

    Alternatively, if you are happy with your way forward, you now have the plan and can start implementation.

You can use this strategy in all areas of your life – in your business, to come up with holiday or fun activities with your family through to whether to move or have an extension for your home. It works on anything where you want to become creative and have a robust and well thought out implementation plan.

Key Learnings

The key learnings from this chapter are:

1. Creativity and flexibility go hand in hand.
2. It is important to be flexible so that when life changes occur, we can adapt more easily.
3. Flexibility is the key to resilience and helps us to discover new ways of doing things in an ever-changing world.
4. The element in the system, who is the most flexible, is the most successful in the system.
5. Use the Disney Creative Strategy to create new innovative ideas in all areas of your life.
6. Remember that the order is important – allow yourself to be creative first, before you think about the plans (realist) or the potential problems (the critic). This will ensure that success is increased and maximised as plans are made and each of the risks are considered to ensure the opportunity is realised.

CHAPTER 13 – GAINING CLARITY OVER DIFFICULT DECISIONS

One of the things you can pretty much guarantee in life is that you will have to make many decisions. Take a moment to think about all the decisions you've made already today – to pick up this book and read, where to sit or stand to read it, what to eat and what to wear.

Sometimes these decisions are easy to make but what happens if those decisions are less than easy? Wouldn't it be lovely to have greater clarity? I love the idea of wisdom. I know it sounds a bit old fashioned but, for me, it is all about having the ability to draw on your experience, gather all the evidence (internal and external), consider all of the options and risks and then take it to a whole different level. In addition, wisdom for me is about connecting all three of our brains. For years, I thought we only had one brain, but neuroscientists have discovered that we have three brains - one in our head, heart and gut (comprised of clusters of neurons). Wisdom is the congruent alignment between all three of these. When we have an aligned connection of our head (logical thinking) to our heart (when it feels right) to our gut feeling (intuition) about a given situation, it can be much easier to make decisions.

Sometimes it's those big decisions that we can find less easy and other times, you've made so many decisions in a row, that the last one is just one too many! For example, when we were building our extension, we had to make decision after decision about where sockets and radiators were to go, the colours of walls and fittings. Each one of these on its own wasn't a big deal but the more decisions we made, the less easy it became to make them! This is where clarity and wisdom can really help because it can reduce stress and, at the end of the day, you're much more likely to stick with your decision.

Sometimes when making decisions, you may feel torn; part of you wants to go in one direction and the other part of you wants the opposite. For example, part of you may want to go to the gym, whereas the other part of you wants to stay in bed. Part of you wants to lose weight whereas another part of you wants to eat chocolate. One of the things to remember is that even if you are procrastinating over a decision, you are still making a decision (i.e. to not make a decision!). It is far more empowering to make active decisions to take your life forward and to be in control of your own destiny, rather than sticking where you are and letting life just evolve whilst hoping for the best!

Activity – Visual Squash

If you have a dilemma and need more clarity, you can use a technique called Visual Squash, which is also sometimes known as Parts Integration. This tool works best when you're working with a dilemma where there are two options which appear to be opposites. For example, you might be trying to decide whether to work for yourself or work for somebody else – for most people there would be an either/or decision to make. With the gym example, part of you may want to go to the gym and part of you may want to stay in bed or maybe you are deciding whether you will live in Scotland or Norfolk – it's less than easy to do both at the same time, so this is where this tool can be really useful.

The first step is to identify the two opposing options. We then go on to discover the positive intention of both of those options and the resources each option brings. As you will remember from the section on the presuppositions of NLP, we already have all the resources we need. This tool gives you a framework to tap into those resources even if they are outside your conscious awareness, so that you can have the wisdom to make a great decision and move forward.

Sometimes you may consciously know what the answer is and other times your unconscious mind will know. Either way is absolutely fine. If the knowledge is unconscious, it is likely that over the following days, weeks or months, you may realise you're moving towards an outcome based on the decision you made unconsciously.

This process uses our visual representational systems to enable us to communicate more easily with our unconscious mind (our storehouse of wisdom) as this is most likely where the answer to the dilemma sits. If the answer was sitting in our conscious mind, we would have already made the decision. In this exercise, we are going to be using symbols or images to represent the two options.

1. When you have thought about the opposing options in your dilemma, check the ecology to make sure it is okay for you to complete this activity today and for you to make this decision, either consciously or unconsciously.

2. As you sit there, place your two hands gently on your lap - ideally you would raise them slightly. Imagine one of the parts (options) is on one of your hands and the other part (option) is on the other. This is where you can create an image or a symbol for each of these parts - create whatever resonates with you.

3. Once you have both parts metaphorically on each hand, you can then decide which part to work with first. Find out the positive intention (by using the chunking technique you have learned before) of the part you want to work with first by asking 'what does (name the part) do for you?' For example, if your dilemma was the one about going to the gym or staying in bed, you would ask 'what does going to the gym do for you?' Notice the response you get and every time you ask the question, move your hand up slightly and repeat the question until you get a higher-level purpose. The higher-level purpose could be love, peace, significance, certainty, fulfilment, safety ... there are a number of possible outcomes.

4. Repeat with the other part, asking the same question, until you reach the same positive intention for both parts.

When you chunk up high enough, you will find a common positive intention. For example, both sides may want love. Once you get to the higher level, you can notice that your hands are at the same level.

5. Once you have discovered this higher-level purpose, you can notice what resources each brings to the situation. For example, maybe one part brings tenacity, perseverance and confidence whilst the other brings self-care and well-being.

6. Once you have noticed all of the resources, slowly move your hands together and as you do so, you can morph the two metaphorical pictures together like the arc of a rainbow to create a new third image. Check this new image is positive as you combine the resources and the aligned positive intention together to create this new super part.

7. Now bring your hands towards your body and let this new image integrate inside of you. Take a moment to curiously explore the solution to your dilemma. You may now have clarity around your next steps or you may feel differently about the decision – either of these options are great as they are taking you a step closer to your outcome.

Examples

There are many examples of how this tool has been used effectively with clients to resolve difficult decisions. One of my clients had the following dilemma – part of them wanted to move and part of them wanted to extend the house. After doing this process, they decided that they were going to stay where they were and make improvements to the house and then move in 5 years.

Another client kept self-sabotaging each time he went for a job interview. Every time, he would do something during the interview that would mean that he wouldn't get the job. This wasn't deliberate and clearly not his conscious intention. Upon investigation, the actual dilemma was that part of him did want a job in America; however, the other part of him wanted to stay in England and be with his family. After doing this process, he decided he would only apply for jobs in locations where his family would want to move. He was then successful during the next interview and moved to New York with his family. Obviously, with this and any process, the ecology step is very important.

Another client wanted to have a family and also wanted a high-flying career. Medically there was nothing wrong, however, she couldn't fall pregnant. After doing this process, she then became pregnant and was able to find a way to do both. Notice with this example that there was nothing consciously or medically stopping her from getting pregnant – the issue, resources and resolution lay within her unconscious mind.

Activity - other decisions – confusion to clarity

The above process and examples are for when there are two options: a dilemma. But what happens when there are lots of options?

A great way to make these kinds of decisions is to use the 'submodality map across process' that we looked at earlier in the book. This uses the principle of how we are storing information and creating those internal representations around the situation. It is a bit like having filing cabinets in your mind – there's a filing cabinet of all those things you're confused about and there's also a filing cabinet for those things that you have clarity about. This process is about putting the confused file into the clarity filing cabinet!

1. Check the ecology of this change – is it okay to make this change in all areas of your life today? Then close your eyes and think about the thing you feel confused about.

2. Create a picture and notice the details of the picture. Note down your answer to these questions.

- Is it black and white or colour?
- Is it near to you or far from you?
- Is it focused or blurry?
- Is it a movie or still?
- Is it framed or panoramic?

3. Notice any sounds that are important.
    - Are they internal or external?
    - What is the volume and tonality?

4. Notice any feelings that are important.
    - Where are they located?
    - Are they internal or external?
    - How intense are they?
    - Is there any movement to these feelings?

5. Open your eyes and do something else for a minute ('break state' – as mentioned before, this is where you think or do something else for a moment so as to disconnect and have some distance from your original thought).

6. Then close your eyes and think about something that is similar in complexity and that you have absolute clarity over. For example, you may struggle with right and left but have complete clarity over east and west. You may use your i-pad with ease but find a new computer system at work really confusing. Provided they are a similar level of complexity, you can use this technique to have a greater feeling of clarity around the old issue.

7. Repeat steps 2, 3 and 4 with the thing you have clarity over, noting the information down as you go.

8. Open your eyes and think about something else for a minute (break state).

9. Now think about the original picture (the one that represented confusion) and change the qualities of this

picture to those that you noted down in step 7. For example, if the 'confused' picture was in black and white but the 'clarity' picture was in colour then you would turn the original confused picture into colour. Repeat for each of the qualities that are different. In essence, we are changing the picture by moving the qualities and details from the 'confused' filing cabinet to the 'clarity' filing cabinet!

10. Notice how you feel now about the old situation that you felt confused by. You may notice you feel different now and that there has been a shift in terms of feeling clearer or you may feel more resilient to embrace the challenge or decision.

Ideally with this process, it is easier to get someone to help you with it by noting down your answers and reading out the changes you need to make or find a trained NLP professional to help you.

These are just a couple of tools you can use to gain clarity and have greater wisdom over decisions.

Key Learnings

The key learnings from this chapter are:

1. We all have multiple decisions to make all the time.
2. If you have a dilemma (i.e. two options) and you don't know which one to go for, then you can use the Visual Squash process.
3. If you are confused about a decision or a situation, then you can change the submodalities of the confused situation to those of something that you have clarity over. This will give you the wisdom to move forward.
4. Remember we are always making decisions … even if we are deciding to not make a decision!

CHAPTER 14 – CHANGE YOUR ATTITUDE, CHANGE YOUR LIFE!

Interestingly, self-care has a lot to do with attitude and mindset (or mind-growth as I prefer to call it). I am sure you have met people who, no matter what happens, focus on the bad things in life: the eternal pessimists. Even when something really good happens, they still manage to find fault.

On the other hand, I am sure you have met people who, no matter what happens, always find a silver lining – something to be happy or grateful about.

Imagine a continuum: a line with optimist at one end and pessimist at the other. Where do you sit on that line? Are you nearer the pessimist or optimist end? Where do you want to be?

The reason this is important in terms of self-care and life in general is that it helps to create our experience of life. When we talked about the NLP Communication Model, we said our meta programs (which create the structure of personality) impact on our filters (deletion, distortion and generalisation). Whether you view a situation pessimistically or optimistically is one of these meta programs. It is, therefore, important to consider carefully where we are on the continuum and where we want to be. Where we are on this continuum will help to create our map of the world – our own unique experience.

Knowing what you now know about the RAS, you can begin to understand why this is so important. When we have an optimistic view on life, that is what we naturally focus on and our RAS will find us more of this. If we are more pessimistic in our view though, this is what our RAS finds for us and we will find ourselves focusing on the negative things in life. It therefore comes down to choice: what do we want out of life and how do we want to create our reality so we can have the life that we desire?

I was brought up around boats. My Dad was a keen sailor and from a very young age, we would be out on the water in a sailing boat. We would hoist the sail and head out on our adventure. Life is a bit like this. Firstly, do we know where we are heading? If not, then we can find ourselves drifting and being buffeted by the wind and waves. We may still get to our destination but it will take longer and the journey may be a bit soggy and not so much fun. With a bit of learning and instruction, however, we can set our direction and start to steer and navigate our way to our destination. The journey becomes more enjoyable and we can become more resilient to manage those less than easy times that life can throw at us. This is what I have found NLP has done for me – given me the instruction to navigate the waters of life more easily.

So, let's look at the different maps, journeys and experiences of the optimist and pessimist. Let us imagine that their life pattern is exactly the same – the same events and the same highs and lows of life.

The pessimist's journey will look something like this. Things are going well – maybe they have got a new job, are going on holiday or getting married. But they get that niggling thought, 'yes, but this won't last'. They don't fully enjoy the time, experience or event as they are always thinking about it ending and how horrible they will feel once it is over. Sure enough, the event does finish and their mood dips. They tell themselves and everybody around them, 'I told you so.' Dwelling on how low they feel, they then wallow in the 'trough' of life for longer. After a while, their mood may start to improve as a new event appears on the horizon. They will slowly move out of the trough but the whole climb is tinged with the thought of how low they have been and even when the good times happen again, they say 'it won't last'. So can you see how their life is playing out? They are missing out on the good times by worrying that they won't last, instead of enjoying the moment. This is an extreme case, however, I do know people that think like this and I'm sure maybe you do too.

At the other end of the spectrum is our optimist. Let's explore what their experience is like. So, we will start at a peak experience – the same event as the pessimist – maybe a holiday, a new job or getting married. At the top of the peak, they are having the best time – enjoying every moment, savouring every detail and being totally present. Then as the event passes, they are still living off the good vibes from the event and starting to look forward to the next great thing that will happen. Optimists tend to be more outcome focused and so have created exciting new goals and outcomes for themselves. Even though they have these goals, they still live in the moment and enjoy life. So, then there is a dip – one of life's troughs. Well, the difference with the optimist is that they know it won't last and say to themselves, 'I'll get through this. I'll learn from it and things will get better.' Guess what their experience is? You guessed it. They move through the trough quicker and move to the good times again sooner than the pessimist.

As you can see, the life events are the same, but their actual experience of life is very different. The pessimist misses the enjoyment of life's highs and spends longer in the troughs of life whereas the optimist spends longer at life's highs and less time in the troughs of life.

So, what do you want your experience of life to be? How do you want the rollercoaster of life to play out? Do you want to enjoy the highs and spend less time in the lows? Or are you finding you are dwelling in the troughs of life?

With this meta program and others (this is just one – there are over 70!), we can find ourselves moving along the continuum rather than always being at one end or the other. There are times when we need to apply a realist filter to make sure we stay safe, for example. However, having an optimistic view of life will start to create a new reality – if that is what you want. With all things in NLP, it is about choice.

So, when you decide you do want to change, what can you do to start to become more optimistic? Well, one of the very simple things to do is to start a gratitude journal – to start to think of all the things you are grateful for. This starts to refocus your RAS and you focus on the optimistic and positive things you already have. You are either reading or listening to this book right now, so you can start to be grateful for your sight or hearing. We can also be grateful for the air we breathe, for the clothes we wear, for the people we care about, for the roof over our head. As you start to think about all the amazing things you have (and often take for granted), you will find more and more things to be grateful for.

Sometimes it takes an event such as the Covid pandemic to make us realise what we previously had - freedom to pop to the shops, to meet with friends or to give someone a hug. When you start focusing on what you have (not what you used to have or want to have), but what you already have and truly feel grateful for, then the law of attraction (with a helping hand from your RAS) will help you find more and more things to be positive and optimistic about.

Optimists will actually find more opportunities because their RAS is looking for positive things to be grateful for. The pessimist may miss these opportunities completely because their focus is on the bad stuff rather than the good stuff they have all around them.

This meta program is very much linked to the belief system of the individual. What does each person believe about their life and themselves? As a generalisation, optimists believe life is good and there are opportunities that they can enjoy. A pessimist, however, believes the opposite. As we have already discovered, beliefs are so important as they create our reality and direct our RAS's focus which will provide evidence of this version of reality. Our filters, which we explored in Chapter 2, also have a part to play as we will delete and distort information to support our beliefs. Let's work through some examples to illustrate this point.

During the Covid pandemic, I know a number of people who were furloughed. Some (the optimists) took the opportunity to do all those things they had been putting off for years – to enjoy the time they had at home, to work on business ideas, to learn something new, to enjoy every moment – knowing they may not have such a length of time at home again whilst still being paid. Others were bored, worried about whether they would have a job or not at the end and allowed the worry to stop them enjoying the time off. Remember worry is a projection of the future. Nobody knows for certain what will happen – so as you know by now, if we are going to project (make things up), we may as well make up something good!

So, as you can see, these two different realities were derived from the same situation. One is productive, proactive and positive and the other less so! Now, I am not saying we should always view life through rose-tinted glasses and just 'believe everything will be okay.' Of course not. What I am saying, however, is that when you have the creativity, flexibility, and a proactive and optimistic approach to life, your RAS will be looking for new opportunities for you. When you choose to learn something, for example, you will have even more skills if you do need to get a new job. If you choose to meet new people, you will have more connections who can help you out. I can't promise you an easy life. However, by taking this attitude, the transition through life's challenges can be easier. You will be more open to notice opportunities, which you may miss when you are focusing on the negatives.

Another thing to remember is whether you are living 'at cause' or 'at effect'. Are you blaming others for things that are happening rather than taking accountability for yourself? If a person is living 'at effect' and blaming others, they are likely to feel out of control and overwhelmed. They will also feel powerless to do anything about it. If, however, you take accountability and ownership for what is happening to you and learn to manage your own response, you will find you can move through situations more easily and become more optimistic in terms of your life and the outcomes you want (remember our equation of Event + Response = Outcome).

In conclusion, your attitude is linked to what you believe about yourself, whether you are blaming others for your life or taking responsibility and whether your glass is half empty or half full.

We all have a choice about life. Start to refocus your RAS to find more positive, optimistic opportunities for yourself. I suggest you start a gratitude journal – add at least 10 new things every day that you are grateful for and notice what happens. Adopting an attitude of optimism will also help you to stretch your map of the world and you will start to surprise yourself as to the incredible world we live in.

Key Learnings

The key learnings from this chapter are:

1. It is not what happens to you that is important but what you do about it.
2. Optimists and Pessimists can have the same events in life but their perception and therefore their reality of life is very different.
3. Optimists enjoy the peaks for longer and move through troughs of life quicker.
4. Pessimists move through the peaks quicker (without fully enjoying them) and remain in the troughs of life for longer.
5. What do you believe about yourself and your reality? Is it supportive or less than helpful?
6. Start to focus on all the things you are grateful for to start to change your perception of reality.

CHAPTER 15 – RELATIONSHIPS THAT MAKE THE WORLD GO ROUND!

We can get through life on our own, of course; however, life is all about relationships – whether that is with your friends, family, loved ones, neighbours, work colleagues or clients. The better the relationships, the better our well-being ... and the opposite is also true.

When we are unhappy in a relationship, this can have a big impact on our well-being and this can filter through to other areas in our lives. If someone is in an unhappy relationship at home, it may impact on their work, their performance levels and, in fact, their relationships with others. So, how do we ensure we can give the relationships that are important to us the best chance of success? We need to decide what is more important – the relationship or being right! Bear in mind that we may think we are right. However, with our knowledge about the NLP Communication Model and how we create our own map of the world, how do we truly know whether we are right or whether they just have a different perspective on life?

So, what can we do to make sure our relationships are the best they can be? We need to think about effective communication, setting boundaries and being curious about the other person's perspective, rather than judging. Remember our brains are projectors rather than cameras. We project our own view of what is right or wrong rather than taking a picture of reality.

How can you become a more effective communicator?

a. Listen to the other person (using all your senses!)

How do we know if the other person has understood our communication the way it was intended? Well, we need to develop what we call sensory acuity to be able to read the other person. We need to become aware of changes in their facial expressions, tone of voice and body language. To be able to notice these changes though, we must first calibrate (notice) what a person looks and sounds like when they understand what we are saying and are in agreement. Then, whenever we communicate with them, we can compare their response to this so that we know how our communication has landed. Are they responding in a congruent way? What I mean by this is, does their body language and tone of voice match what they are saying? Sometimes (especially when the individual lacks confidence or wants to please others), they may say they understand and agree when actually they may not. Once you are able to notice this, you can then communicate your message again in a different way so that it is received in the way you intended.

These changes in tonality or facial expressions may be very slight. When we are listening intently and actively to what the other person is saying (rather than planning on what we are going to say next or thinking about something else altogether), we are more likely to notice these nuances and respond to them. Remember the NLP Presupposition: you can't not communicate – so even if you are sitting there thinking that you are not communicating ... you are.

The other benefit of listening in this way is that when you listen to what they say, they may have a better idea than the one you had originally thought of!

b. Take responsibility for the way that your communication is received by the other person

Remember, it is our responsibility to ensure our message lands correctly – that it is received in the way that it was intended. If the response we get isn't what we expected, it is our responsibility to do something about it, rather than to say it's their fault for not understanding properly. Living 'at cause' means taking responsibility for our communication. We need to check that the other person understands what we mean, rather than assuming and later finding out that they have a different interpretation of the message than we did.

If you are communicating with someone and you notice the response that you get isn't the one you anticipated, what do you do next? Well, you can become curious and go around to their side in order to understand their perspective, rather than expecting them to come around to your side. You can be flexible and change the way you communicate.

Let me give you an example. I came home late from training the other evening and my husband was in the kitchen cooking dinner. He was making a salad while the curry was cooking. I walked in, said 'hi' and as I was chatting went over to the curry and gave it a stir. From his reaction, I could tell that what I had thought I was communicating (a kind and helpful gesture) wasn't quite how he had experienced it! Instead of responding with irritation, I asked, 'What did you think I meant by stirring the curry?' He said that he felt I had come in and taken over as he wasn't doing it right. I could then understand why he was less than impressed! By understanding where he was coming from first, I was able to explain that my intention was to be helpful because I had got home late and he was having to cook (yet again). So instead of having an argument, we carried on cooking together and this has never happened again since.

So, if the response to your communication isn't what you expect, go around to their side, understand their perspective and then change the way you communicate to ensure that your message has landed the way you intended. Most relationships would be much easier if we all adopted this way of being – curiosity rather than judgement. I'm not saying it is always easy. Like most things though, the more you do it, the easier it becomes and the results are definitely worth it.

I talked about mindreading in Part One. It is also important to not expect others to mind-read what you are thinking. In other words, expecting others to know what you need or mean without actually telling them. For example, if you are upset about something, rather than expecting your partner to know what you are upset about, you may need to actually tell them!

c. Build rapport with the other person

What happens if there is still resistance even after you have gone around to their side? Well, resistance is a sign of lack of rapport. We need to learn to build rapport with those we care about to have better relationships. When we talk about rapport, we are talking about that feeling we have when we are in sync with another person and are on the same wavelength. We feel that they are like us, understand us and trust us. Communication then becomes so much easier.

How can we build rapport? Well, there are a number of different ways:
- Match their body language by sitting in the same way as they are, or even mirroring them (as if seeing a reflection in a mirror).
- Match or mirror them in miniature. For example, you could cross your arms as they cross their legs.
- Match the speed and volume at which they speak, the words they use or tone of voice.
- Match subtle movements such as a slight tilt of the head.

You can always test whether you are in rapport by doing something and seeing if they follow, such as taking a drink or changing your posture.

However, the best and easiest way to build rapport, in my view, is to give the other person your undivided attention – to really listen to what is going on for them.

So, why is rapport so important? Well, it is all about trust. We trust people that we are in rapport with. First though, you need to be flexible yourself – you can't expect the other person to change to be like you; you need to meet them in their map of the world rather than expect them to meet you in yours.

You can do this by pacing and leading – pace the other person's experience until you are in rapport and then lead them to a place of understanding or resourcefulness. Let me give you an example. Have you ever phoned a call centre and been really angry? Maybe the company owe you money or have been unhelpful. If the person that you talk to tells you to calm down and speaks in a very slow and calm voice, how does that make you feel? If you are anything like me, it can make you feel even more annoyed as it can seem like they are not listening. It makes me feel that they are not in rapport with me. In fact, it can feel like they are deliberately breaking rapport.

Let's use this pacing and leading technique. Imagine you are the call centre employee. You need to go around your client's side first to build rapport. Pace your client by matching the speed of their voice. Maybe increase your volume slightly so you are just under the volume they are using and increase your energy (again to just under the level they are at). Say something like, 'Okay so let me understand what you are saying more fully so I can help you to resolve this.' They will be far more likely to be receptive than if you tell them to calm down (this can be like a red rag to a bull!).

Once you are in rapport, you can start to lead the client. Slowly move to a lower volume and gradually slow your speed. As they become calmer, you can begin to help them solve their issue and bring them to a good outcome.

Now, I know some people may think this is a lot of hard work just to communicate a message. Like anything, the first few times you do it, you may have to think about it consciously and then after a while, it will become second nature – an unconscious competence.

How can you improve communication with someone you find less than easy?

First, train your RAS to focus on the positive aspects of that person. Think about what you like about that person ... however hard that may be to start with. Find 5 things you like about them or that you are grateful for. This will start to help your RAS to focus on finding more good things rather than bad or annoying things.

It is also useful to notice if the actions of others are triggering an emotional response for you. If you are finding the behaviour of someone annoying or upsetting, spend some time exploring what is happening for you – do you see yourself in them (even if you don't want to admit it!)? Is there something within you that you want to change?

You can also change your internal representation of them by changing the submodalities of the internal movie in your mind. Close your eyes for a moment and imagine that person. Note down the answers to these questions:

- Do you have a picture? If so, how big is the picture?
- Where is it?
- Is it black and white or in colour?
- Is it a movie or still picture?
- Is it framed or panoramic?
- Is it in focus?
- Is the focus changing?
- Are there sounds that are important? If so, where are they coming from?
- What is the volume?
- What is the pitch of the sound? Is it a high pitch or a low pitch?
- Are there any feelings that are important? If so, how intense are they? Where are the feelings located?
- Is the person at their current age?
- Are they smiling or looking cross?

These questions help you to look at the submodalities you hold around that person – the qualities or details of the internal representation. As we have seen in Part One, when we change the submodalities around a person or a situation, our feelings can also change.

Start to play around with the submodalities. For example, if the picture is far away, you could move it nearer and see if this is better or worse for you. If it was in black and white, you could make it colour and see if that changes it. Basically, what you are doing is playing with the internal representation you have of that person.

As you know, we store images in our unconscious minds. Therefore, each time we think of a person we find 'difficult', we unconsciously access the image or movie that makes us feel that way.

You could also identify the submodalities of someone you like in the same way as above and then compare that to the details you have around someone you don't like – that will give you a good indication of what I am talking about.

The great thing is that we can change the internal representation of a person, should we want to. So, if you find someone at work less than easy to get on with and have a less than helpful internal representation of that person, you could change the qualities slightly and notice the difference.

As you know, our internal representation has a big impact on how we feel (our state) which impacts on our behaviour towards that person, so if you want to improve a relationship, then think about the internal representation you hold about the person and start to make changes – if they look angry in your picture, change their expression to a smile and see what happens!

In relationships, it is important to care for ourselves as well as others. Some people are not good for us. Remember, we do have a choice. If a person isn't good for our health, we can choose to limit or eliminate the amount of time we spend with them.

How can you support somebody going through a less than easy time?

Being empathetic rather than sympathetic can really help.

Empathy is about being there to support and understand the

other person and helping them to find a way forward when they want to move on.

Activity – Perceptual Positions

We've talked a lot in this chapter about the importance of considering things from the other person's perspective.

The final tool I want to share with you in this chapter is called Perceptual Positions and is a great NLP tool for really stepping into another person's shoes. We use this phrase often but how often do we truly do this? So often, as humans, we are still just seeing things through our own biased perspective.

This tool will enable you to have better relationships with those who are important to you – whether that is with someone who you have a less than easy relationship with or someone who you have a good relationship with and want to make even better.

This process needs to be completed on your own (without the other person present) as it is important for you to be open and say exactly what is on your mind to enable you to get a resolution. It will allow you the space to explore the relationship and gain a different perspective on the situation to enable you to move forward in a proactive and considered manner.

1. You will need to have some space for this. Place 4 sheets of paper on the floor. Label the first as 'self' and place that opposite the second sheet of paper which you need to label as 'other' (the person you want to have a better relationship with). These should be placed as if at the 12 and 6 positions on a clock. Then, on the third sheet, write 'learning position' and place this at 3 o'clock. Label the final sheet as the 'wise position' and place it opposite the 'learning position' at 9 o'clock. So, in essence, you have created a square with 'self' and 'other' at opposite corners and 'learning position' and 'wise position' in the other corners.

2. Step into the 'self' position and say all you want to say to the other person about the relationship – say exactly how you feel.

3. Once you have said everything you want to say, step into the 'learning position' and gather the positive learnings from what you have just experienced. You may have gained a different perspective from being able to speak in this way. By stepping out of the 'self' position and taking a disassociated learning position, you gain a new perspective. Again, something we don't do that often.

4. Before you step into the 'other' position, take a moment to consider the other person and think about their background, their situation, their history and where they are coming from (their map of the world). Once you have taken time to do this, step into the 'other' position and take on their countenance and their posture. Speak in response to what you heard being said in the 'self' position. Speak as though you are them (use 'I' not 'you'). Again, just say out loud whatever comes. Take your time in this position saying everything you want to say.

5. Step back into the 'learning position'. As before, in this disassociated position, notice all the learnings that you can gather from what was said in the 'other' position.

6. You are now going to step into the 'wise' position. You can decide who the 'wise' person is that you want to step into the shoes of … who do you respect in terms of their wisdom? It can be anyone – real or imagined – but it needs to be someone who you respect and would listen to.

   Step into the 'wise' position. Take on that persona. Having observed the interaction between 'self' and 'other', allow the wise person to speak their wisdom - whatever comes to mind in terms of advice they would give and what observations they noticed. Seeing the situation from a wise outsider's view, can give you a fresh perspective.

7. Step back into the 'learning position'. From this position, you can gather the new learnings you have gained from the 'wise' position. You can now also gather together all the learnings from all the positions.

8. Step back into 'self' position and notice how that feels different. Notice how you want to behave differently now... maybe you want to say something new to the other person. Maybe you now have the wisdom to know how to communicate and interact with them in the future.

You can always go around the process again if you feel there is more to learn. The idea is for you to get to a position where you have the wisdom and the learnings from all the positions to enable you to move forward with the relationship in a fresh way.

This is a great process and worth taking the time over as it can help to transform important relationships in a safe environment.

So, in conclusion, we all need support – whether from friends, family, work colleagues or neighbours. In all relationships, there is an element of give and take; balance is key for a healthy relationship. If you are finding you are giving more than you are receiving, then it could be time to decide how much you value the relationship and maybe set yourself some boundaries, so you are not taken advantage of. If, however, you find you are taking more than giving in a relationship, think about how you can start to give more – this will help restore the balance.

Key Learnings

The key learnings from this chapter are:

1. The meaning of the communication is the response you get … if it isn't the one you expected, you need to change your approach.
2. You are responsible for landing your communication effectively. Therefore, you need to have flexibility to see things from their perspective first, rather than expect them to come to yours.
3. To build effective relationships, you need to pace and lead. Meet them where they are emotionally and then help them to come to a more resourceful state.
4. Build rapport to reduce resistance.
5. Empathy rather than sympathy builds strong relationships.
6. Ensure you have boundaries where necessary and a balance between giving and taking.
7. Look after the relationships that are important to you. This may need some work and time … and it is worth every moment.
8. Do things for others – this will help them, as well as help you, to feel good.
9. You can use the Perceptual Position process to improve relationships that are important to you.
10. Update your internal representation of people you find less than easy and notice the difference that this makes.

CHAPTER 16 – CREATING YOUR EXCITING FUTURE

In this chapter, we are going to start to look at the possibilities for your future. What do you want your future to look like? We have already talked about well-formed outcomes in terms of achieving particular goals. We are now going to look at the bigger picture in terms of creating the future you want and achieving your life's purpose.

When we talk about purpose here, we are talking about creating a life you truly desire, which is full of meaning for you, and enables you to become the best version of yourself (see Chapter 8). It could be something which is beyond you - benefiting the wider environment or community. Those people who have the greatest satisfaction in life tend to feel they have something valuable to offer to make the world a better place in some way – whether that is by helping a neighbour or creating new and innovative ideas! It is about giving to other people and doing something which will give you a sense of purpose.

So, I would encourage you to start to think about your life and the qualities, skills and empowering beliefs that you now have and start to envision what your life could look like. You could use the Disney Creativity Strategy (Chapter 12) to help you to do this.

What could you do? What would that purpose be which would excite you? What would get you jumping out of bed in the morning? Using NLP, you can start to visualise what your life could look like and the experiences you would like to have in the future that will enable you to live a rich, meaningful life.

Once you have visualised the kind of future you want, you can use a model created by Robert Dilts called Neurological Levels to make sure that you have everything in place to help you get there. It can help you to identify the level at which you are operating and can help you to identify the level where you may need to make changes.

Dilt's Logical Levels of Change

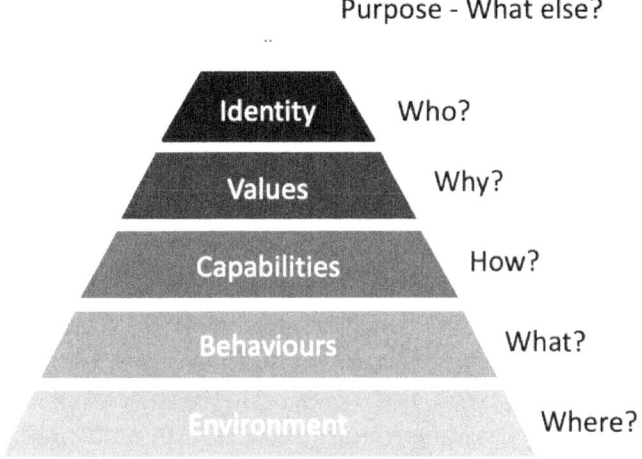

Purpose - What else?

Identity — Who?
Values — Why?
Capabilities — How?
Behaviours — What?
Environment — Where?

'Purpose' is something that is bigger than just yourself and gives you ... yes, you guessed it ... purpose!

'Identity' refers to those qualities and characteristics which make you you!

'Values and Beliefs' (as discussed in previous chapters) determine why we do what we do and relate to what we believe and what is important to us.

'Capabilities' are those things that we can learn to do.

'Behaviours' are what you say and do. We have already covered in this book how you can change these when they are not working for you.

'Environment' refers to physical environment – whether that is work or home.

For you to achieve greatness in your life, reach your full potential and feel genuinely fulfilled, all these elements need to support one another. The lower levels need to be aligned to the higher levels to ensure congruence and a feeling of certainty and confidence. The levels at the top of the pyramid are the most powerful. Therefore, when we make changes to our purpose, for example, there will be a ripple effect which will filter down to the lower levels, bringing it into alignment. However, when you change the bottom level, this may not necessarily change the top ones. My recommendation is to look at each level in isolation at first and then in connection with the other layers in the diagram.

You can look at each logical level in turn in relation to your vision for the future. For example, who do you need to be to enable this to happen? What qualities and characteristics do you need? What values and beliefs will you need to have? What skills will you need? What will you need to learn to enable this to happen? What will you be saying and doing? Are there any behaviours you need to change that are holding you back? What decisions will you need to make? (Chapter 13) What environment would support you and your vision? (See Chapter 9 on space).

For example, maybe through creating a well-formed outcome you decide that you want to become a coach. You can use this model to increase your chances of success – to ensure that you have what you need at each level to achieve that goal:

- 'Purpose' - this could be to help others within your workplace or community. It is important that this is something you are passionate about and that you will find fulfilling.
- 'Identity' - to be a coach you will need to be empathetic, supportive, compassionate, focused and enthusiastic.
- 'Values and Beliefs' - to be a coach you will need to believe in yourself and that what you are doing makes a difference. Your values (those things that are important to you) could include integrity, honesty and trust.
- 'Capabilities' - could include becoming an NLP professional and gaining coaching skills and experience.
- 'Behaviours' - could include what you say and do during the sessions.

- 'Environment' - could include an online coaching platform or a private space.

By considering each level in this way, you can identify if there are any gaps. What do you need to do to fill those gaps to enable you to achieve your desired outcome?

Dilts' Logical Levels is a great model that you can use in business as well as in your private life to have congruence within and through each level. There will be overlaps – what you believe about yourself, for example, will play out in your home and work life, so making changes will benefit both areas. If you feel you are a different person at work than at home and you want more consistency and alignment, this model is useful for identifying where you are out of alignment. You can then make changes by using the tools I have shared with you in this book.

As you start visualising your exciting future, you will discover more and more about yourself. Discovering yourself is like peeling an onion – you peel off one layer and there is another underneath for you to discover! This is why people call it a journey rather than a destination. Continued personal and professional development is like training to be an athlete. Athletes don't exercise to peak fitness and then give up saying, 'I am now fit!' They continue to train. The same goes for personal and professional development. Reading a book is just the start – it is the continued learning and regular application of what you have learnt that will ultimately enable you to become the best version of yourself.

As well as planning your exciting future, you may also start to realise that you can enjoy life more right now. Being present and grateful for all you have already achieved will bring you greater peace and satisfaction in the here and now. In my experience, when you come from a place of peace, love and satisfaction (rather than coming from a place of stress and striving), your future becomes easier. Again, this book can help you to start to make those changes.

Another key message I would love you to take away from this book is this: you always have choice. You can choose your emotions and your behaviours. When someone says or does something you don't like, it doesn't have to 'make' you feel bad. You can use the tools I have shared with you to enable you to choose how you respond and have a better outcome. We are all in control of ourselves – I'm in control and responsible for me and you for you! So, if the outcome you are experiencing isn't one you want, use those tools I have shared with you to make those changes, so you have a different outcome.

If your current situation is not what you want, you can do one of three things: remove yourself from it, accept it or change yourself. The latter enables your perspective to change and thereby change how you feel about it.

You can see this as an opportunity to spend some time deciding what you want your future to look like. We only have one life. I am not saying it will always be easy gliding – there will always be curve balls in life. However, as we have learnt, it is not what happens to you that is important but how you respond. By using these tools, you will be able to bounce back quicker.

Using these tools and techniques and being curious to stretch your 'map of the world' will enable you to see the world through a different perspective; there is so much more to life than what we are experiencing right now. An exciting adventure awaits as you start to truly discover your own greatness. You can be the catalyst for change, as Ghandi said, 'be the change you wish to see in the world'.

Rather than feeling that life 'does stuff to you', you are in the pilot's seat and can start to take ownership of the direction of travel, to create the life that inspires you and you can truly enjoy living.

With this power, comes great responsibility so use the ecology checks you have learnt in this book to ensure that you have considered the consequences of any change (as well as any secondary gains) so that you can easily move from where you are now to where you want to be. You may already be happy with where you are - if so, excellent. You can use these tools to enjoy the ride even more, make your life even easier and have even more joy, peace and contentment along the way!

Remember, the only person you can guarantee you will be with for the rest of your life is you, so it's important to like and love yourself and create the life you really want.

Key Learnings

The key learnings from this chapter are:

1. Use Robert Dilts' Neurological Levels to become more aligned in your goals and decisions.
2. When you can't change the situation, change yourself.
3. The more you change, the more you discover about yourself.
4. Ensure you consider the consequences of the changes you make – you are not an island!
5. Remember, you always have choice.
6. The only person you are guaranteed to be with for all of your life is you.
7. Working on yourself is the greatest and most powerful gift you can give yourself.

CHAPTER 17 – FINAL THOUGHTS

Firstly, thank you for reading this book. I trust there have been some tips and tools that you can apply within your life to enable you to move towards your goals and achieve greatness more easily.

My intention for this book is to inspire you to discover how incredible you already are. By understanding the power of performance psychology and applied neuroscience, you can discover your true potential and know that you have even more resources than you ever dreamed of to create the life you desire.

This book is really just giving you a taster of what NLP is all about. The real experience and transformation comes when you apply these tools and I really do recommend you go on a course, so as to experience first-hand what NLP is and become even more familiar with some of the concepts I have talked about.

This book touches lightly on a number of subjects … there is always lots more to learn and NLP provides such a powerful toolkit to enable us to make changes easily and navigate through life's adventures more smoothly.

When you want to continue your NLP journey, I would love to share more with you. My training school is based in the UK, and I run a number of courses where you can discover first hand your own unique potential.

In closing, I want to wish you all the best in your journey. Enjoy applying the techniques I have shared with you and I would love to hear how you are progressing. So, enjoy the flight, be kind to yourself and remember to master the controls of your life!

ABOUT THE AUTHOR

So, why NLP? When I discovered it in 2010, it answered the questions I had had for many years, as well as those questions that I hadn't even known to ask! To say it was life changing for me is an understatement. It gave me a different perspective on life, relationships, work, family, friends – the list is endless. Since I learnt about it, I have used it in every area of my life and it has become part of who I am.

It is my absolute passion to share NLP with as many people as I can. It was like someone had shared with me the best kept secret in the world – how to have better relationships, how to improve the quality of my life, how to be more successful, how to have more choice over my behaviours, emotions and beliefs and how to change things that weren't working for me. It gave me the answers, insights and tools to make the change – to take back the controls of my life and to start to fly my plane in the direction I wanted it to go, rather than being buffeted around at the mercy of the weather.

Now, I am not saying that I have had a perfect life since; however it has given me a set of tools and ways of thinking to be able to manage life more easily and to come out of less than easy situations more quickly and effectively. It isn't a miracle cure but it gives some powerful insights that can enable you to make changes in your life, when you want to.

If your life is perfect, that's great – you can still use NLP to become even greater!

In my experience, I have found that there is always more to learn and change. The day I think that I have 'cracked it' is the day I know nothing! We are all a work in progress – it is just easier to have the handbook for how to create an awesome life, rather than flying blind and hoping we will get to our destination. Someone said recently that their idea of hell is getting to the end of their life and realising what they could have been compared to what they were – an interesting thought, that's for sure. This is why I love to keep learning, sharing and evolving to enable me (as my young friend so eloquently put it) 'to live my best life'.

It is now my mission in life to spread the power of NLP far and wide – to help you to live a happier and more fulfilled life. I do this through my company, Achieve Your Greatness Ltd (School of NLP). The way I run my business is like a family – once you have trained with us, you are part of the family (if you choose to be).

I create a safe, supportive and fun space for you to discover who you REALLY are once all the 'shoulds' and 'musts' and 'have tos' have been removed. I will support you to look deep inside yourself and ask yourself THAT question: what do I really want? And I will teach you the tools and techniques to get there.

Alongside my NLP training certifications, I have over 30 years' business experience in the public and private sector, an MBA (Masters Degree in Business Administration) and an ILM Level 7 Certificate in Executive Coaching and Mentoring. That means that I approach my training with insight and strategy gleaned from multiple industries and disciplines.

I am here to help you achieve your greatness, so please visit www.achieveyourgreatness.co.uk to find out more about NLP courses and coaching.

Thanks again for reading my book and enjoy the flight of your life with NLP!

Emma x

Printed in Dunstable, United Kingdom

66562078R00100